GENOCIDE **&** PERSECUTION

I Cambodia

Titles in the Genocide and Persecution Series

GENOCIDE & PERSECUTION

I Cambodia

Jeff Hay
Book Editor

Frank Chalk
Consulting Editor

GREENHAVEN PRESS
A part of Gale, Cengage Learning

GALE
CENGAGE Learning·

Detroit • New York • San Francisco • New Haven, Conn • Waterville, Maine • London

Elizabeth Des Chenes, *Director, Publishing Solutions*

© 2013 Greenhaven Press, a part of Gale, Cengage Learning

Gale and Greenhaven Press are registered trademarks used herein under license.

For more information, contact:
Greenhaven Press
27500 Drake Rd.
Farmington Hills, MI 48331-3535
Or you can visit our Internet site at gale.cengage.com.

For product information and technology assistance, contact us at:

Gale Customer Support, 1-800-877-4253
For permission to use material from this text or product, submit all requests online at
www.cengage.com/permissions

Further permissions questions can be emailed to permissionrequest@cengage.com

Every effort is made to ensure that Greenhaven Press accurately reflects the original intent of the authors. Every effort has been made to trace the owners of copyrighted material.

Cover image © Bobby Fisher/Corbis.
Interior barbed wire artwork © f9photos, used under license from Shutterstock.com.

LIBRARY OF CONGRESS CATALOGING-IN-PUBLICATION DATA

Cambodia / Jeff Hay, book editor.
    p. cm. -- (Genocide and persecution)
    Includes bibliographical references and index.
    ISBN 978-0-7377-6252-5 (hardcover)
1. Genocide--Cambodia 2. Political atrocities--Cambodia. 3. Political violence--Cambodia 4. Crimes against humanity--Cambodia. 5. Communism--Cambodia--History. 6. Human rights--Cambodia. 7. Cambodia--Politics and government--20th century. I. Hay, Jeff.
    DS554.8.C355 2013
    959.604'2--dc23

                                                                              2012026607

Printed in the United States of America
1 2 3 4 5 6 7 16 15 14 13 12

Contents

Chapter 2: Controversies Surrounding the Cambodian Genocide

Chapter 3: Personal Narratives

Preface

> *"For the dead and the living, we must bear witness."*
>
> Elie Wiesel, Nobel laureate and
> Holocaust survivor

T he histories of many nations are shaped by horrific events involving torture, violent repression, and systematic mass killings. The inhumanity of such events is difficult to comprehend, yet understanding why such events take place, what impact they have on society, and how they may be prevented in the future is vitally important. The Genocide and Persecution series provides readers with anthologies of previously published materials on acts of genocide, crimes against humanity, and other instances of extreme persecution, with an emphasis on events taking place in the twentieth and twenty-first centuries. The series offers essential historical background on these significant events in modern world history, presents the issues and controversies surrounding the events, and provides first-person narratives from people whose lives were altered by the events. By providing primary sources, as well as analysis of crucial issues, these volumes help develop critical-thinking skills and support global connections. In addition, the series directly addresses curriculum standards focused on informational text and literary nonfiction and explicitly promotes literacy in history and social studies.

Each Genocide and Persecution volume focuses on genocide, crimes against humanity, or severe persecution. Material from a variety of primary and secondary sources presents a multinational perspective on the event. Articles are carefully edited and introduced to provide context for readers. The series includes volumes on significant and widely studied events like the Holocaust, as well as events that are less often studied, such as the East Pakistan genocide in what is now Bangladesh. Some volumes focus on multiple events endured by a specific people, such as the Kurds, or multiple events enacted over time by a particular oppressor or in a particular location, such as the People's Republic of China.

Each volume is organized into three chapters. The first chapter provides readers with general background information and uses primary sources such as testimony from tribunals or international courts, documents or speeches from world leaders, and legislative text. The second chapter presents multinational perspectives on issues and controversies and addresses current implications or long-lasting effects of the event. Viewpoints explore such topics as root causes; outside interventions, if any; the impact on the targeted group and the region; and the contentious issues that arose in the aftermath. The third chapter presents first-person narratives from affected people, including survivors, family members of victims, perpetrators, officials, aid workers, and other witnesses.

In addition, numerous features are included in each volume of Genocide and Persecution:

- An annotated **table of contents** provides a brief summary of each essay in the volume.
- A **foreword** gives important background information on the recognition, definition, and study of genocide in recent history and examines current efforts focused on the prevention of future atrocities.
- A **chronology** offers important dates leading up to, during, and following the event.
- **Primary sources**—including historical newspaper accounts, testimony, and personal narratives—are among the varied selections in the anthology.
- **Illustrations**—including a world map, photographs, charts, graphs, statistics, and tables—are closely tied

to the text and chosen to help readers understand key points or concepts.

- **Sidebars**—including biographies of key figures and overviews of earlier or related historical events—offer additional content.

- **Pedagogical features**—including analytical exercises, writing prompts, and group activities—introduce each chapter and help reinforce the material. These features promote proficiency in writing, speaking, and listening skills and literacy in history and social studies.

- A **glossary** defines key terms, as needed.

- An annotated list of international **organizations to contact** presents sources of additional information on the volume topic.

- A **list of primary source documents** provides an annotated list of reports, treaties, resolutions, and judicial decisions related to the volume topic.

- A **for further research** section offers a bibliography of books, periodical articles, and Internet sources and an annotated section of other items such as films and websites.

- A comprehensive subject **index** provides access to key people, places, events, and subjects cited in the text.

The Genocide and Persecution series illuminates atrocities that cannot and should not be forgotten. By delving deeply into these events from a variety of perspectives, students and other readers are provided with the information they need to think critically about the past and its implications for the future.

Foreword

The term *genocide* often appears in news stories and other literature. It is not widely known, however, that the core meaning of the term comes from a legal definition, and the concept became part of international criminal law only in 1951 when the United Nations Convention on the Prevention and Punishment of the Crime of Genocide came into force. The word *genocide* appeared in print for the first time in 1944 when Raphael Lemkin, a Polish Jewish refugee from Adolf Hitler's World War II invasion of Eastern Europe, invented the term and explored its meaning in his pioneering book *Axis Rule in Occupied Europe*.

Humanity's Recognition of Genocide and Persecution

Lemkin understood that throughout the history of the human race there have always been leaders who thought they could solve their problems not only through victory in war, but also by destroying entire national, ethnic, racial, or religious groups. Such annihilations of entire groups, in Lemkin's view, deprive the world of the very cultural diversity and richness in languages, traditions, values, and practices that distinguish the human race from all other life on earth. Genocide is not only unjust, it threatens the very existence and progress of human civilization, in Lemkin's eyes.

Looking to the past, Lemkin understood that the prevailing coarseness and brutality of earlier human societies and the lower value placed on human life obscured the existence of genocide. Sacrifice and exploitation, as well as torture and public execution, had been common at different times in history. Looking toward a more humane future, Lemkin asserted the need to punish— and when possible prevent—a crime for which there had been no name until he invented it.

Legal Definitions of Genocide

On December 9, 1948, the United Nations adopted its Convention on the Prevention and Punishment of the Crime of Genocide (UNGC). Under Article II, genocide

> means any of the following acts committed with intent to destroy, in whole or in part, a national, ethnical, racial or religious group, as such:
>
> (a) Killing members of the group;
>
> (b) Causing serious bodily or mental harm to members of the group;
>
> (c) Deliberately inflicting on the group conditions of life calculated to bring about its physical destruction in whole or in part;
>
> (d) Imposing measures intended to prevent births within the group;
>
> (e) Forcibly transferring children of the group to another group.

Article III of the convention defines the elements of the crime of genocide, making punishable:

> (a) Genocide;
>
> (b) Conspiracy to commit genocide;
>
> (c) Direct and public incitement to commit genocide;
>
> (d) Attempt to commit genocide;
>
> (e) Complicity in genocide.

After intense debate, the architects of the convention excluded acts committed with intent to destroy social, political, and economic groups from the definition of genocide. Thus, attempts to destroy whole social classes—the physically and mentally challenged, and homosexuals, for example—are not acts of genocide under the terms of the UNGC. These groups achieved a belated but very significant measure of protection under international criminal law in the Rome Statute of the International Criminal

Court, adopted at a conference on July 17, 1998, and entered into force on July 1, 2002.

The Rome Statute defined a crime against humanity in the following way:

> any of the following acts when committed as part of a widespread and systematic attack directed against any civilian population:
>
> (a) Murder;
>
> (b) Extermination;
>
> (c) Enslavement;
>
> (d) Deportation or forcible transfer of population;
>
> (e) Imprisonment or other severe deprivation of physical liberty in violation of fundamental rules of international law;
>
> (f) Torture;
>
> (g) Rape, sexual slavery, enforced prostitution, forced pregnancy, enforced sterilization, or any other form of sexual violence of comparable gravity;
>
> (h) Persecution against any identifiable group or collectivity on political, racial, national, ethnic, cultural, religious, gender . . . or other grounds that are universally recognized as impermissible under international law, in connection with any act referred to in this paragraph or any crime within the jurisdiction of this Court;
>
> (i) Enforced disappearance of persons;
>
> (j) The crime of apartheid;
>
> (k) Other inhumane acts of a similar character intentionally causing great suffering, or serious injury to body or to mental or physical health.

Although genocide is often ranked as "the crime of crimes," in practice prosecutors find it much easier to convict perpetrators of crimes against humanity rather than genocide under domestic laws. However, while Article I of the UNGC declares that countries adhering to the UNGC recognize genocide as "a crime under international law which they undertake to prevent and to punish," the Rome Statute provides no comparable international mechanism for the prosecution of crimes against humanity. A treaty would help individual countries and international institutions introduce measures to prevent crimes against humanity, as well as open more avenues to the domestic and international prosecution of war criminals.

The Evolving Laws of Genocide

In the aftermath of the serious crimes committed against civilians in the former Yugoslavia since 1991 and the Rwanda genocide of 1994, the United Nations Security Council created special international courts to bring the alleged perpetrators of these events to justice. While the UNGC stands as the standard definition of genocide in law, the new courts contributed significantly to today's nuanced meaning of genocide, crimes against humanity, ethnic cleansing, and serious war crimes in international criminal law.

Also helping to shape contemporary interpretations of such mass atrocity crimes are the special and mixed courts for Sierra Leone, Cambodia, Lebanon, and Iraq, which may be the last of their type in light of the creation of the International Criminal Court (ICC), with its broad jurisdiction over mass atrocity crimes in all countries that adhere to the Rome Statute of the ICC. The Yugoslavia and Rwanda tribunals have already clarified the law of genocide, ruling that rape can be prosecuted as a weapon in committing genocide, evidence of intent can be absent when convicting low-level perpetrators of genocide, and public incitement to commit genocide is a crime even if genocide does not immediately follow the incitement.

Several current controversies about genocide are worth noting and will require more research in the future:

1. Dictators accused of committing genocide or persecution may hold onto power more tightly for fear of becoming

vulnerable to prosecution after they step down. Therefore, do threats of international indictments of these alleged perpetrators actually delay transfers of power to more representative rulers, thereby causing needless suffering?

2. Would the large sum of money spent for international retributive justice be better spent on projects directly benefiting the survivors of genocide and persecution?

3. Can international courts render justice impartially or do they deliver only "victors' justice," that is the application of one set of rules to judge the vanquished and a different and laxer set of rules to judge the victors?

It is important to recognize that the law of genocide is constantly evolving, and scholars searching for the roots and early warning signs of genocide may prefer to use their own definitions of genocide in their work. While the UNGC stands as the standard definition of genocide in law, the debate over its interpretation and application will never end. The ultimate measure of the value of any definition of genocide is its utility for identifying the roots of genocide and preventing future genocides.

Motives for Genocide and Early Warning Signs

When identifying past cases of genocide, many scholars work with some version of the typology of motives published in 1990 by historian Frank Chalk and sociologist Kurt Jonassohn in their book *The History and Sociology of Genocide*. The authors identify the following four motives and acknowledge that they may overlap, or several lesser motives might also drive a perpetrator:

1. To eliminate a real or potential threat, as in Imperial Rome's decision to annihilate Carthage in 146 BC.

2. To spread terror among real or potential enemies, as in Genghis Khan's destruction of city-states and people who rebelled against the Mongols in the thirteenth century.

3. To acquire economic wealth, as in the case of the Massachusetts Puritans' annihilation of the native Pequot people in 1637.

4. To implement a belief, theory, or an ideology, as in the case of Germany's decision under Hitler and the Nazis to destroy completely the Jewish people of Europe from 1941 to 1945.

Although these motives represent differing goals, they share common early warning signs of genocide. A good example of genocide in recent times that could have been prevented through close attention to early warning signs was the genocide of 1994 inflicted on the people labeled as "Tutsi" in Rwanda. Between 1959 and 1963, the predominantly Hutu political parties in power stigmatized all Tutsi as members of a hostile racial group, violently forcing their leaders and many civilians into exile in neighboring countries through a series of assassinations and massacres. Despite systematic exclusion of Tutsi from service in the military, government security agencies, and public service, as well as systematic discrimination against them in higher education, hundreds of thousands of Tutsi did remain behind in Rwanda. Government-issued cards identified each Rwandan as Hutu or Tutsi.

A generation later, some Tutsi raised in refugee camps in Uganda and elsewhere joined together, first organizing politically and then militarily, to reclaim a place in their homeland. When the predominantly Tutsi Rwanda Patriotic Front invaded Rwanda from Uganda in October 1990, extremist Hutu political parties demonized all of Rwanda's Tutsi as traitors, ratcheting up hate propaganda through radio broadcasts on government-run Radio Rwanda and privately owned radio station RTLM. Within the print media, *Kangura* and other publications used vicious cartoons to further demonize Tutsi and to stigmatize any Hutu who dared advocate bringing Tutsi into the government. Massacres of dozens and later hundreds of Tutsi sprang up even as Rwandans prepared to elect a coalition government led by moderate political parties, and as the United Nations dispatched a small international military force led by Canadian general Roméo Dallaire to oversee the elections and political transition. Late in 1992, an international human rights organization's investigating team detected the hate propaganda campaign, verified systematic massacres of Tutsi, and warned the international community that Rwanda had already entered the early stages of genocide, to no avail. On April 6, 1994, Rwanda's genocidal killing accelerated at an alarming pace when someone shot down the airplane flying Rwandan president Juvenal Habyarimana home from peace talks in Arusha, Tanzania.

Hundreds of thousands of Tutsi civilians—including children, women, and the elderly—died horrible deaths because the world ignored the early warning signs of the genocide and refused to act. Prominent among those early warning signs were: 1) systematic, government-decreed discrimination against the Tutsi as members of a supposed racial group; 2) government-issued identity cards labeling every Tutsi as a member of a racial group; 3) hate propaganda casting all Tutsi as subversives and traitors; 4) organized assassinations and massacres targeting Tutsi; and 5) indoctrination of militias and special military units to believe that all Tutsi posed a genocidal threat to the existence of Hutu and would enslave Hutu if they ever again became the rulers of Rwanda.

Genocide Prevention and the Responsibility to Protect

The shock waves emanating from the Rwanda genocide forced world leaders at least to acknowledge in principle that the national sovereignty of offending nations cannot trump the responsibility of those governments to prevent the infliction of mass atrocities on their own people. When governments violate that obligation, the member states of the United Nations have a responsibility to get involved. Such involvement can take the form of, first, offering to help the local government change its ways

through technical advice and development aid, and second—
if the local government persists in assaulting its own people—
initiating armed intervention to protect the civilians at risk. In
2005 the United Nations began to implement the Responsibility
to Protect initiative, a framework of principles to guide the international community in preventing mass atrocities.

As in many real-world domains, theory and practice often
diverge. Genocide and crimes against humanity are rooted in
problems that produce failing states: poverty, poor education,
extreme nationalism, lawlessness, dictatorship, and corruption.
Implementing the principles of the Responsibility to Protect doctrine burdens intervening state leaders with the necessity of addressing each of those problems over a long period of time. And
when those problems prove too intractable and complex to solve
easily, the citizens of the intervening nations may lose patience,
voting out the leader who initiated the intervention. Arguments
based solely on humanitarian principles fail to overcome such
concerns. What is needed to persuade political leaders to stop
preventable mass atrocities are compelling arguments based on
their own national interests.

Preventable mass atrocities threaten the national interests of
all states in five specific ways:

1. Mass atrocities create conditions that engender widespread and concrete threats from terrorism, piracy, and
   other forms of lawlessness on the land and sea;
2. Mass atrocities facilitate the spread of warlordism, whose
   tentacles block affordable access to vital raw materials
   produced in the affected country and threaten the prosperity of all nations that depend on the consumption of
   these resources;
3. Mass atrocities trigger cascades of refugees and internally
   displaced populations that, combined with climate change
   and growing international air travel, will accelerate the
   worldwide incidence of lethal infectious diseases;

4. Mass atrocities spawn single-interest parties and political agendas that drown out more diverse political discourse in the countries where the atrocities take place and in the countries that host large numbers of refugees. Xenophobia and nationalist backlashes are the predictable consequences of government indifference to mass atrocities elsewhere that could have been prevented through early actions;

5. Mass atrocities foster the spread of national and transnational criminal networks trafficking in drugs, women, arms, contraband, and laundered money.

Alerting elected political representatives to the consequences of mass atrocities should be part of every student movement's agenda in the twenty-first century. Adam Smith, the great political economist and author of *The Wealth of Nations*, put it best when he wrote: "It is not from the benevolence of the butcher, the brewer, or the baker that we expect our dinner, but from their regard to their own interest." Self-interest is a powerful engine for good in the marketplace and can be an equally powerful motive and source of inspiration for state action to prevent genocide and mass persecution. In today's new global village, the lives we save may be our own.

Frank Chalk

Frank Chalk, who has a doctorate from the University of Wisconsin-Madison, is a professor of history and director of the Montreal Institute for Genocide and Human Rights Studies at Concordia University in Montreal, Canada. He is coauthor, with Kurt

Jonassohn, of The History and Sociology of Genocide *(1990); coauthor with General Roméo Dallaire, Kyle Matthews, Carla Barqueiro, and Simon Doyle of* Mobilizing the Will to Intervene: Leadership to Prevent Mass Atrocities *(2010); and associate editor of the three-volume Macmillan Reference USA* Encyclopedia of Genocide and Crimes Against Humanity *(2004). Chalk served as president of the International Association of Genocide Scholars from June 1999 to June 2001. His current research focuses on the use of radio and television broadcasting in the incitement and prevention of genocide, and domestic laws on genocide. For more information on genocide and examples of the experiences of people displaced by genocide and other human rights violations, interested readers can consult the websites of the Montreal Institute for Genocide and Human Rights Studies (http://migs.concordia.ca) and the Montreal Life Stories project (www.lifestoriesmontreal.ca).*

World Map

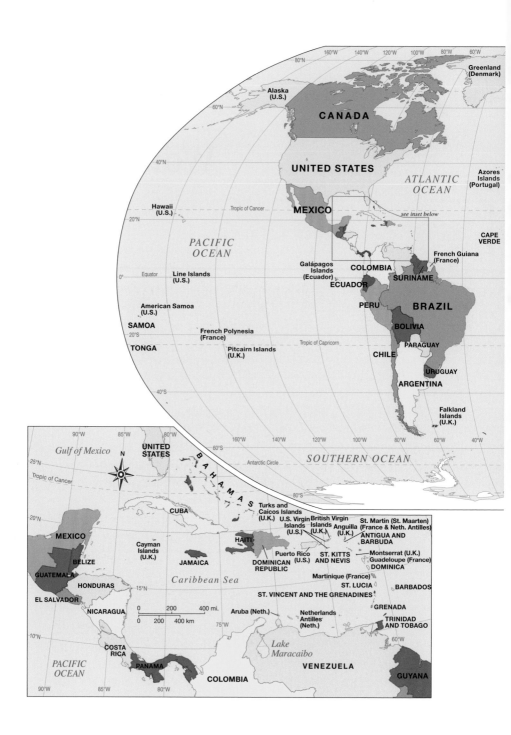

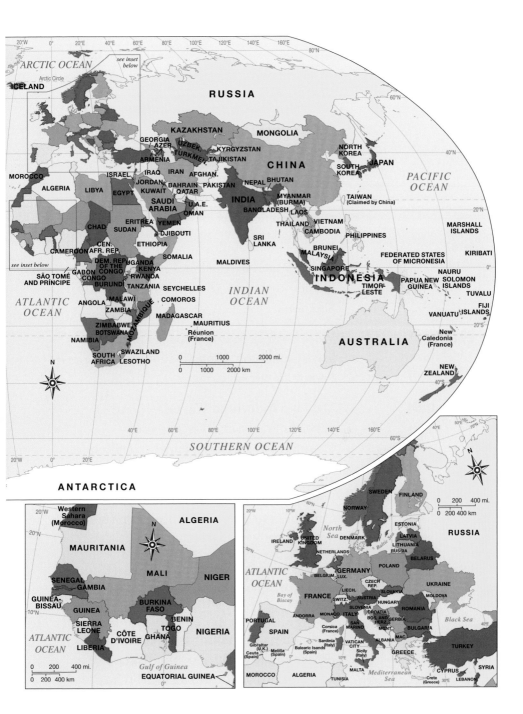

Chronology

Ninth–Fourteenth Centuries	During this time period, the era of the Khmer Empire takes place in modern Cambodia.
1864	Cambodia becomes a French colony that is eventually enlarged to include modern-day Vietnam and Laos. The colony is known as French Indochina.
1941	Japan occupies Indochina during its World War II expansion. In Cambodia, it rules together with King Norodom Sihanouk.
1945	World War II ends and the Japanese leave Cambodia. King Sihanouk asks the French to return.
1946–1954	The First Indochina War takes place between France and Vietnamese Communists and independence fighters under leader Ho Chi Minh.
1949	Pol Pot, then known as Saloth Sar, leaves Cambodia to study in France. He returns in 1953.
1953	King Sihanouk gains a limited degree of independence for Cambodia from France.
1954	Vietnamese Communists defeat the French in the First Indochina War. Negotiations divide the former French Indochina into four states: Cambodia,

Laos, North Vietnam, and South Vietnam.

1955   Sihanouk gives up his throne in favor of his father, but remains the head of the government in Cambodia.

1961   Seeking to defend South Vietnam from incursions from the Communist North, the United States sends increasing numbers of military advisors and trainers to the region.

1963   Pol Pot becomes the head of the Communist Party of Kampuchea, formed in 1960. Sihanouk eventually gives it the familiar name "Khmers Rouge," or Red Khmers. Khmer refers to the Cambodian ethnicity and the country's main language, while Rouge is the French word for "red," or Communist.

1965   The United States begins to send regular combat troops to South Vietnam. By 1968 there are more than half a million US troops in the region.

King Sihanouk breaks off diplomatic relations with the United States and eventually allows Vietnamese Communists the use of border areas for transport routes as well as the use of the seaport of Sihanoukville.

1969   The United States expands its large-scale bombing campaigns to Cambodian border regions used by Vietnamese Communists as supply routes.

1970	The Cambodian government is overthrown by General Lon Nol. Sihanouk forms an opposition force, which includes the Khmer Rouge.
	The ground war in Vietnam expands into Cambodia.
1970–1975	Lon Nol's regime tries to defend itself against both North Vietnamese Communists and the growing Khmer Rouge movement. Meanwhile, US bombing raids in border regions continue until 1973.
April 17, 1975	Khmer Rouge forces take the capital, Phnom Penh, sealing their control over the country. They order the evacuation of the city.
April 30, 1975	The war in Vietnam ends with a Communist conquest of the southern capital, Saigon.
1976	Pol Pot becomes the formal head of the Khmer Rouge's Democratic Kampuchea after King Sihanouk resigns.
	Purges continue of those in society considered undesirable by the Khmer Rouge.
1977	Pol Pot, Ieng Sary, Nuon Chea, and other leaders cement their authority by purging political enemies.
	The secretive Pol Pot makes his first public announcement to the nation.
	Border conflicts with Communist Vietnam increase tensions between the two countries.

December 25, 1978	Vietnam launches a full invasion of Democratic Kampuchea.
January 7, 1979	Vietnamese troops capture Phnom Penh.
January 8, 1979	A new Cambodian government under Heng Samrin is declared. It makes clear its friendship with Vietnam. Now on the run but still large, the Khmer Rouge begins a long war against both the Vietnamese and Cambodian factions loyal to the Vietnamese from bases along the Thai-Cambodia border.
1989	The Vietnamese occupation of Cambodia ends.
1991	A United Nations agreement provides for the presence of a UN peacekeeping force in Cambodia and prepares the way for elections.
1993	Cambodia's first election since the Khmer Rouge results in a coalition government of Hun Sen, a former Khmer Rouge cadre, and King Sihanouk. The Khmer Rouge boycotts the election.
1997	Pol Pot is ousted as the leader of the Khmer Rouge.
April 15, 1998	Pol Pot dies in a jungle hideaway.
1999	The last Khmer Rouge fighters surrender to the coalition government.
2007	After years of legal wrangling, the United Nations and the Hun Sen government

agree on principles for trials of surviving Khmer Rouge leaders.

2009

Kaing Guek Eav, or "Duch," commander of the notorious S-21 killing and torture center in Phnom Penh, is sentenced by the UN tribunal to thirty-five years in prison. That sentenced is extended to life imprisonment in 2012.

2011–2012

Trials of "Brother Number Two" Nuon Chea, President Khieu Samphan, and Foreign Minister Ieng Sary continue in Phnom Penh.

CHAPTER 1

Historical Background on the Cambodian Genocide

Chapter Exercises

	Cambodia
Total area	181,035 sq km World ranking: 90
Population	14,952,665 (urbanized population 20% of total) World ranking: 68
Ethnic groups	Khmer 90%, Vietnamese 5%, Chinese 1%, Other (including Cham Muslims) 4%
Religions	Buddhism 96.4%, Islam 2.1%, Other 1.3%
Literacy (total population)	73.6% Male: 84.7% Female: 64.1%
GDP	$33.89 billion (2011 estimate) World ranking: 107 GDP per capita: $2,200 World ranking: 186

Source: *The World Factbook.* Washington, DC: Central Intelligence Agency, 2012. www.cia.gov.

1. Analyzing Statistics

Question 1: Cambodia is a small and fairly homogenous country, meaning that the great majority of its people share ethnicity and religion. Does this help explain why the Khmer Rouge targeted ethnic and religious minority groups?

Question 2: As its GDP and economic ranking indicate, Cambodia is one of the poorest countries in Asia. Did poverty have anything to do with the rise of the Khmer Rouge? Have the lasting effects of the Cambodian genocide held back the country's economic growth?

Question 3: Compare the literacy rate of Cambodian men to Cambodian women. Do you think the fact that less than one quarter of the population is urbanized helps explain this?

2. Writing Prompt

Write an article describing what went on at S-21, the notorious torture and killing center also known as Tuol Sleng. Consider who was in charge, some of the methods used, and what happened to most of the victims who passed through S-21. Make sure it has a strong title that grabs the readers' attention.

3. Group Activity

Form into small groups. One group should examine what life was like for soldiers of the Khmer Rouge, another group should investigate what happened to victims of the Khmer Rouge, and another should explore how outsiders tried to learn what occurred during the Cambodian genocide. Each group should then prepare a brief, five-minute speech on its findings.

The Khmer Rouge Movement in Cambodia

Ben Kiernan

The genocide in Cambodia was carried out by a radical Communist regime known as the Khmer Rouge from 1975 to 1979. In the following viewpoint, a scholar describes the origins of the Khmer Rouge, its rise to power in the wake of the Vietnam War, its brutal control, and its slow dissolution in the 1980s and 1990s. The author examines the roles of Khmer Rouge leaders such as Pol Pot and Ieng Sary, and he describes how their regime targeted both Cambodians and ethnic minorities. Ben Kiernan is a professor of history at Yale University and director of Yale's Cambodian Genocide Program.

Cambodia's Prince Norodom Sihanouk coined the term *Khmer Rouge* in the 1960s to describe his country's then heterogeneous, communist-led dissidents, with whom he allied after his 1970 overthrow. More precisely, he called them *Khmers rouges* in French, *khmaer kraham* in Khmer [the Cambodian language] both meaning "Khmer Reds." In 1975, the Khmer Rouge leadership, secretly headed by Pol Pot, took power, pushed the Prince aside, and established the Democratic Kampuchea regime (DK).

Ben Kiernan, "Khmer Rouge," *Encyclopedia of Genocide and Crimes Against Humanity*, 1st ed., vol. 2. New York: Macmillan Reference USA, 2005, pp. 608–613. Copyright © 2005 by Cengage Learning. All rights reserved. Reproduced by permission.

Origins of Communism in Cambodia

Cambodian communism first emerged in 1930 as part of a multinational anti-French independence movement, the Indochina Communist Party (ICP), which extended throughout what was then French Indochina. In 1951, the Vietnamese communist leader, Ho Chi Minh, separated the ICP into national branches. In Cambodia, the ICP set up the Khmer People's Revolutionary Party (KPRP). Its members, especially former Buddhist monks, led the nationwide Khmer Issarak ("independence") movement. They adopted for its flag a silhouette of the medieval temple of Angkor Wat: five towers on a red background. A faction of the movement made early use of the name "Democratic Kampuchea." An anti-KPRP group flew a flag with a three-towered Angkor motif which would later become the emblem of the DK regime. Members of another anti-communist splinter group perpetrated portentous racial massacres, targeting minority Vietnamese residents in 1949 and Cham Muslims in 1952. A Cambodian student in Paris named Saloth Sar, then calling himself the "Original Khmer," returned home in 1953 and served briefly in the communist-led Issarak ranks. He later assumed the *nom de guerre* ["name of war," or pseudonym] "Pol Pot."

The First Indochina War ended with the 1954 Vietnamese victory over the French at Dien Bien Phu. The Geneva settlement brought Cambodia full independence under Prince Sihanouk, who soon adopted a foreign policy of cold war neutrality. That was, in part, an accommodation to the communists' internal challenge, implicitly acknowledging both their role in the independence war and their potential to disrupt a more pro–United States regime. Neutrality also served an international strategy to keep Cambodia out of the escalating conflict in neighboring Vietnam.

The Changing of the Vanguard

Radicals of both the left and the right, dissatisfied with Sihanouk's domestic and foreign policies, had to bide their time, head for the hills, or leave for Vietnam or Thailand. Half of Cambodia's Issarak veterans took up exile in Hanoi [city in Vietnam]. Most of the remaining grassroots leftists were either mollified by Sihanouk's neutrality, jailed by his police, or disappeared, like the underground Cambodian communist leader, Tou Samouth, who was mysteriously killed in 1962. At that point a group of younger, Paris-educated militants headed by Saloth Sar, Ieng Sary, and Son Sen quickly assumed top leadership positions within the debilitated KPRP. Of these, only Sar had previously been a member of the three-person Standing Committee of the party's Central Committee; in 1960 he had been named No. 3, ranking third in that three-person body. Now, however, Saloth Sar and Ieng Sary ranked first and third in an expanded Standing Committee of five members. Former students occupied the first, third, fifth, sixth, and eleventh ranks in the Central Committee of twelve.

With the support of ICP veteran Nuon Chea, who became Sar's second in command, the younger cohort now dominated both the Standing Committee and the Central Committee, referring to themselves as the "Party Center" (*mocchim paks*). Technically this was a codeword for the Central Committee, but henceforth, the latter rarely if ever met. Quietly abandoning their teaching jobs in the capital for rural redoubts, the party's new leadership launched it onto the offensive, changing its name to the Communist Party of Kampuchea (CPK) in 1966.

The veteran party leaders had been from rural and Buddhist backgrounds, and were pro-Vietnamese though relatively moderate. However, they were mostly replaced by younger, urban, French-educated, anti-Vietnamese extremists headed by "the Original Khmer," Pol Pot. Ieng Sary and Son Sen were both Khmer Krom, natives of Vietnam's Mekong Delta, and were resentful of the Vietnamese majority there. From the jungles of Cambodia's remote northeast, these new CPK leaders planned an armed rebellion against Sihanouk's independent regime, ignoring his neutral nationalism and labeling him a U.S. puppet.

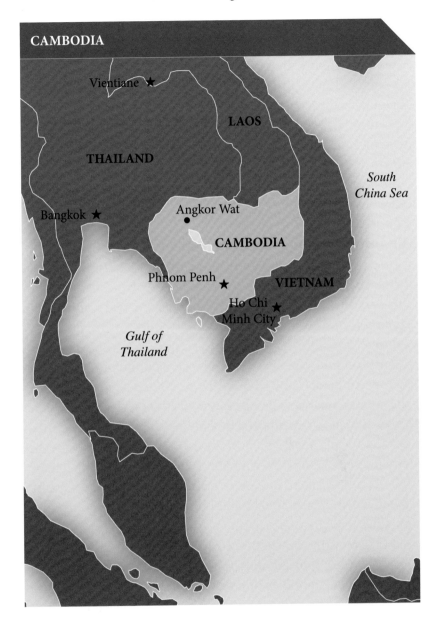

Sihanouk sensed the threat and cracked down on all leftists, driving above-ground moderates into the arms of the younger militants who were leading the CPK. Sihanouk began denouncing other "Khmers Rouges," especially three prominent elected politicians: Khieu Samphan, Hou Yuon, and Hu Nim. In 1967, they too joined the rural underground.

Accompanying them into clandestine opposition came a new generation of disgruntled youth who had benefited from Sihanouk's rapid post-independence expansion of educational opportunities, but had failed to secure commensurate employment in a fragile economy that grew in the period spanning 1963 to 1965 and remained plagued by corruption. Young rural school teachers and students soon comprised the bulk of "Khmer Rouge" cadres [fighters and officials].

The Impact of the Vietnam War on Cambodia

In 1967, the CPK Center launched a limited insurgency, which provoked repression by the Cambodian Army. Sihanouk's regime was also unable to handle the Vietnam War's impacts on Cambodia, from plunging national revenues to the politically explosive presence of Vietnamese communist troop sanctuaries. General Lon Nol overthrew Prince Sihanouk on March 18, 1970, and allied Cambodia with the United States. From his exile in Beijing, the Sihanouk quickly joined forces with the Khmer Rouge insurgents, led by Pol Pot's shadowy CPK Center. Lon Nol's army massacred thousands of the country's ethnic Vietnamese residents, driving 300,000 more to flee to Vietnam. This set a precedent for later "ethnic cleansing" by the CPK Center, which began attacking its Vietnamese-communist military allies in September 1970.

Both sides in the Vietnam conflict treated Cambodia as a theater of their ground and air war. United States aerial bombardments of Cambodia's border areas, begun in March 1969, escalated across the country until August 1973. American aircraft dropped over half a million tons of bombs on rural Cambodia, killing over 100,000 peasants and driving many survivors into the insurgent ranks.

This triggered a second wave of Khmer Rouge rural recruitment. On May 2, 1973, the Directorate of Operations of the U.S.

Central Intelligence Agency reported the results of its investigations in Kandal province:

1. Khmer Insurgent (KI [Khmer Rouge]) cadre have begun an intensified proselyting [*sic*] campaign among ethnic Cambodian residents in the area of Chrouy Snao, Kaoh Thom district, Kandal province, Cambodia, in an effort to recruit young men and women for KI military organizations. They are using damage caused by B-52 strikes as the main theme of their propaganda. The cadre tell the people that the Government of Lon Nol has requested the airstrikes and is responsible for the damage and the "suffering of innocent villagers" in order to keep himself in power. The only way to stop "the massive destruction of the country" is to remove Lon Nol and return Prince Sihanouk to power. The proselyting [*sic*] cadres tell the people that the quickest way to accomplish this is to strengthen KI forces so they will be able to defeat Lon Nol and stop the bombing.

2. This approach has resulted in the successful recruitment of a number of young men for KI forces. Residents around Chrouy Snao say that the propaganda campaign has been effective with refugees and in areas of Kaoh Thom and Leuk Dek districts which have been subject to B-52 strikes.

CPK internecine purges also accelerated during the U.S. bombardment. Portending the genocide to come, and while secretly, systematically killing off nearly all one thousand Khmer Issarak communist returnees from Hanoi, in 1973 and 1974 the Center stepped up CPK violence against ethnic Vietnamese civilians. It also purged and killed ethnic Thai and other minority members of the CPK's Western and Northeast Zone committees, banned an allied group of ethnic Cham Muslim revolutionaries in the East, and instigated severe repression of Muslim communities. Other victims of the Center included its former

A militiaman stands guard at Angkor Wat in 1981. The area served as a hiding place during the Khmer Rouge reign. The twelfth-century complex has been both a Hindu and Buddhist temple and is now a UNESCO World Heritage Site. © Wilber E. Garret/National Geographic/ Getty Images.

Sihanoukist allies, moderate local communists, and more independent Marxists such as Hou Yuon, a popular Paris-educated intellectual who had differed with Pol Pot. Yuon was marginalized, then murdered in 1975. The Center sponsored the CPK Southwest and Northern Zone military commanders, Chhit Choeun (alias "Mok") and Ke Pauk, in their purges of suspected rivals and opponents there. CPK moderates were concentrated in the Eastern Zone, where regional differences remained evident as late as 1977.

The U.S. Congress ended the American bombardment on August 15, 1973. The opposing Cambodian armies fought out the last two years of the war, with continuing large-scale U.S. military assistance to Lon Nol's Republican forces based in the cities, and sporadic Vietnamese aid to the Khmer Rouge dominating the rural areas, which the CPK termed its "bases" (*moultanh*).

The Khmer Rouge Takes Over

On April 17, 1975, Khmer Rouge armies entered Phnom Penh [Cambodia's capital]. The new state was formally re-named Democratic Kampuchea (DK) the following January. CPK Secretary-General Pol Pot headed the regime as DK's Prime Minister. He and the other members of the CPK Center who moved into the capital comprised the regime's effective national leadership. They included the CPK Standing Committee members Nuon Chea (Deputy CPK Secretary), Vorn Vet, Ieng Sary, and Son Sen (hierarchically ranked three, five, and eight, respectively) who served as Deputy Prime Ministers for the Economy, Foreign Affairs, and Defense. Also among the leadership was Khieu Samphan, who ranked number nine and served as DK's head of state. In the rural Zones, in concert with the Center, Southwest, and Northern military chiefs Mok (who ranked seventh in the Standing Committee hierarchy) and Ke Pauk (ranking thirteenth still outside the Standing Committee, but a member of the CPK Central Committee) gained increasing power as they consolidated the CPK's victory, executed its enemies, and purged its regional administrations. Mok and Pauk later became National Chief and Deputy Chief of the army's General Staff. Two other CPK Standing Committee members, So Phim and Moul Sambath (numbers four and six in the hierarchy), ran the Eastern and Northwest Zones, but held no comparable national posts.

Immediately upon victory, the CPK labeled the two million conquered urban dwellers "new people" (*neak thmei*), driving them in all directions from the capital and other cities. It forcibly settled townspeople among the rural "base people" (*neak moultanh*) who had lived in the countryside during the 1970–1975 war, and put them to work in agricultural labor camps without wages, rights, or free time. Before the rice harvest of late 1975, the CPK Center again rounded up 800,000 of these urban deportees from various regions and dispatched them to the Northwest Zone, doubling its population. Tens of thousands died of starvation there during 1976, while the regime began exporting rice. Meanwhile, the CPK hunted down, rounded up, and killed thousands of Lon Nol's defeated Khmer Republic officials, army officers, and increasingly, soldiers, schoolteachers, and alleged "pacification agents" (*santec sampoan*) who, in most cases, had merely protested the repression or just the rigorous living conditions imposed on them. By early 1979, approximately 650,000 people, or one quarter of the "new" Khmer, died from execution, starvation, overwork, disease, and denial of medical care.

The Khmer Rouge revolution had won initial support among the peasant "base people," but they, too, were rewarded with a life of unpaid collective labor. The CPK regime prohibited rights to land, freedom of religion, and family life. Meals were served in plantation-style communal mess halls. Couples were separated, and youths were drafted into the workforce, army, or militia. Many peasant children were trained to spy on their parents, and to kill suspected "enemies" such as former city dwellers, "CIA" and "KGB agents," recalcitrants, and alleged malingerers. In 1976 and 1977, the CPK Center and its security apparatus, the *Santebal* supported by Mok's and Pauk's divisions, conducted massive new purges of the Northwest and Northern Zone CPK administrations, arresting and killing tens of thousands of peasants who were related to the purged local officials. Starvation and repression escalated nationwide in 1977 and especially in 1978. By early 1979, 675,000 Khmer "base people" (15% of the *neak moultanh*) had perished from execution or other causes like starvation, for which CPK policies were responsible.

Pol Pot claimed to be "four to ten years ahead" of other Asian communist states, adding: "We have no model in building up our new society." This disguised the Maoism [China's revolutionary communism] in the CPK's call for a "Super Great Leap Forward," the influence of Stalinism [from the Soviet Union], and even that of the French Revolution [1789–1799] which DK copied by introducing a ten-day working week (with one-day weekends). The CPK exported agricultural and forest products, including rare tropical fauna, to China in return for its massive military assistance program. In all, imposing these policies by force caused the deaths of 1.7 million Cambodians.

The Center charged that local and national veteran communists, who were more moderate and favored "a system of plenty" over the DK regime's policies, with being corrupted by "a little prosperity," neglectful of ideology, and "taken to pieces" by material things. Its Santebal purged and killed prominent national-level communists like Keo Meas in 1976, Hu Nim in 1977, and So Phim, Moul Sambath, and even Vorn Vet in 1978, all the while asserting increasingly tight control of Zone and Region committees. By 1978 the Santebal had executed over half the members of the CPK Central Committee, accusing most of involvement in fantastic plots hatched by a hostile new troika [group of three]: "the CIA, the KGB, and the Vietnamese." Deuch [or Duch, originally named Kaing Guek Eav], the commandant of the Santebal's central prison, "S-21" or Tuol Sleng, incarcerated and executed 14,000 Khmer Rouge members and others, leaving only seven survivors.

The Khmer Rouge Regime Committed Genocidal Persecution

The Center's severe repression of the majority Khmer rural population and its Stalin-like massive purge of the party were accompanied by intensified violence against ethnic minorities, even among the "base people," escalating the patterns of 1973–1975. In mid-1975, the new CPK regime expelled from Cambodia more than 100,000 Vietnamese residents. In the next four years, more than half of the nation's ethnic Chinese, 250,000 people, perished in the Cambodian countryside, the greatest tragedy ever to befall Southeast Asia's Chinese diaspora. In late 1975, the CPK ferociously repressed a Cham Muslim rebellion along the Mekong River. Pol Pot then ordered the deportation of 150,000 Chams living on the east bank of the Mekong, and their forced dispersal throughout the Northern and Northwest Zones. In November 1975, a Khmer Rouge official in the Eastern Zone complained

to Pol Pot of his inability to implement "the dispersal strategy according to the decision that you, Brother, had discussed
with us." Officials in the Northern Zone, he complained, "absolutely refused to accept Islamic people," preferring "only pure
Khmer people." Santebal communications, available through the
Documentation Center of Cambodia, show that Northern Zone
leader Ke Pauk sent a message to Pol Pot two months later, in
which he listed "enemies" such as "Islamic people." Deportations
of Chams began again in 1976, and by early 1979, approximately
100,000 of the country's 1975 Cham population of 250,000 had
been killed or worked to death. The 10,000 ethnic Vietnamese
remaining in the country were all hunted down and murdered in
1977 and 1978. Oral evidence suggests that the ethnic Thai and
Lao minorities were also subjected to genocidal persecution.

Meanwhile the Khmer Buddhist monks were decimated in
a nationwide CPK campaign to repress "reactionary religion,"
banned by DK's 1976 Constitution. A Center document stated
in September 1975: "Monks have disappeared from 90 to 95 percent . . . Monasteries . . . are largely abandoned . . . the cultural
base must be uprooted." Of a total of 2,680 monks in a sample of
8 of Cambodia's 3,000 monasteries in 1975, only 70 monks were
found to have survived to 1979. If this toll could be extrapolated
to the other monasteries, as few as 2,000 of the country's 70,000
Buddhist monks may have survived. That constitutes a prima fa-
cie [authentic] case of genocide of a religious group.

Vietnam Invades Cambodia

Most of the CPK's victims came from the majority Khmer population, and the major resistance it faced was in the East. From late
1976, accelerating the purges of regional administrations, the
Santebal and Center army units subjected all five regions of the
Eastern Zone to concerted waves of arrests and massacres of local CPK officials and soldiers. These reached a crescendo on May
10, 1978, when Phnom Penh Radio broadcast a call not only to
"exterminate the 50 million Vietnamese" but also to "purify the

The Angkor Empire

Hundreds of years ago one of the great empires in Asia was based in Cambodia. Known variously as the Khmer Empire, the Angkor Empire, or simply Angkor, it controlled much of mainland Southeast Asia from the ninth through the fourteenth centuries. It was a military power and a center of the Buddhist religion, and it left behind the great temple known as Angkor Wat, which stands today at the center of a vast city of ruins in northwestern Cambodia near the city of Siem Reap.

The Khmer Empire was established by King Jayavarman II, who reigned from 792 to 850 AD. His successors expanded the territory under their control, and began a program of monumental building that reflected both their growing power and their version of Buddhism, which was heavily influenced by Hinduism from India. King Suryavarman II built Angkor Wat in the twelfth century, consecrating it to the Hindu god Vishnu. King Jayavarman III established a capital city and religious center nearby called Angkor Thom where stood a massive temple known as the Bayon featuring the carving of many different versions of the face of Buddhist figure Avalokitesvara. Meanwhile, the prosperity of the empire was based on a productive rice crop as well as fish from the nearby inland sea known as the Tonle Sap, and the city grew large enough to support a population of one million people.

Enemies began to chip away at the territory of the Angkor Empire in the twelfth century. First the Chams, from modern-day Vietnam, and then the emerging state of Siam, or Thailand, began to present major military challenges, carving away territory steadily. Mismanagement of water resources, and therefore a dwindling rice crop, is also thought to have weakened the empire. Although people still continued to live around Angkor Wat and Angkor Thom by the end of the fourteenth century, the Khmer Empire was no longer a major regional power. For its part, Angkor Wat and the ruins around were eventually abandoned as living spaces. They served as battlegrounds and hiding places during Cambodia's wars and upheavals in the 1970s and 1980s and in the 1990s and 2000s became one of Asia's great tourist attractions.

masses of the people" of Cambodia. Khmer Rouge officers in the Eastern Zone mutinied two weeks later. Pol Pot's divisions were unable to crush them quickly. One and one-half million easterners were now branded as "Khmer bodies with Vietnamese minds" (*kbal yuon khluon khmaer*). Center forces massacred between 100,000 and 250,000 people in six months. Of the 1.7 million dead in less than four years of CPK rule, more than 500,000 had been deliberately murdered.

The Eastern Zone rebels, led by Heng Samrin and Chea Sim, fought back for several months before retreating across the Vietnamese border, where they requested aid and joined earlier Khmer Rouge rebels and defectors like Hun Sen. Hanoi was ready to intervene. Beginning in early 1977, Phnom Penh had mounted brutal cross-border attacks on Thailand, Laos, and especially Vietnam, slaughtering thousands of both Vietnamese and Khmer Krom there. On December 25, 1978, 150,000 Vietnamese troops launched a multipronged assault and took the Cambodian capital on January 7, 1979. They drove the CPK forces, including Pol Pot and most Center leaders, to the Thai border.

The dissident Khmer Rouge commanders established a new communist-led regime in Phnom Penh. Former regimental officer Hun Sen, who had defected to Vietnam in mid-1977, became Foreign Minister. Promoted to Prime Minister in 1985, he began a limited liberalization which accelerated in 1989. After UN-organized elections in 1993, Hun Sen became Second Prime Minister in a coalition with Sihanoukist party leader Prince Norodom Ranariddh. But Pol Pot's 10,000-strong rump Khmer Rouge army, revived during the 1980s by international assistance and enjoying sanctuary in Thailand, posed a continuing threat on the northwestern border.

The Khmer Rouge movement finally began to unravel in August 1996. First, in return for a "pardon," Ieng Sary defected to the Cambodian government with the military units under his command. Other Khmer Rouge leaders sought similar treatment from Phnom Penh. In June 1997, fearing further betrayal, Pol Pot murdered Son Sen. In the jungle of northern Cambodia, as the last military forces loyal to Pol Pot evacuated their headquarters, they drove their trucks over the bodies of Son Sen, his wife Yun Yat—the former DK minister of culture—and a dozen family members. Mok turned in pursuit, arrested Pol Pot, and subjected him to a show trial in the jungle. But in March 1998, Pauk led a new mutiny against Mok and defected to the government. Pol Pot died the next month. Then, in December 1998, Nuon Chea and Khieu Samphan abandoned Mok and surrendered to the Cambodian government. They said they were now "sorry" for the crimes they had perpetrated. In 1999, the Cambodian army captured Mok and arrested the former Center security chief, Deuch. As of May 2004, they remained in jail awaiting trial.[1]

Note

1. Mok died while imprisoned in 2006, before being brought to trial. Deuch was convicted of crimes against humanity, murder, and torture by the Extraordinary Chambers in the Courts of Cambodia in 2010 and is serving a sentence of life imprisonment.

The Early Khmer Rouge Destroyed Many Enemies and Laid the Groundwork for Further Development

Pol Pot et al.

In the following viewpoint, the leader of the Khmer Rouge issues a report in late 1976, the second year of the regime's control in Cambodia. He emphasizes the work the Khmer Rouge has already done to "purify" Cambodian society but recognizes that the task is not yet completed. The leader of the Khmer Rouge was a somewhat mysterious figure who called himself Pol Pot. Born under the name of Saloth Sar in 1925, Pol Pot received a technical education in France, where he also took part in meetings of radical Communists. In the 1960s he emerged as a leader of Cambodia's radical Communists, bent on separating them from the Communist Party of neighboring Vietnam, an old enemy of Cambodia. After Pol Pot's Khmer Rouge forces took command of the capital of Cambodia in April 1975, he became "Brother Number One," the top official in a new and very radical regime.

As far as the tasks of the socialist revolution are concerned, we have raised them thoroughly and properly and we have

"Report of the Activities of the Party Center According to the General Political Tasks of 1976," *Pol Pot Plans the Future: Confidential Leadership Documents from Democratic Kampuchea, 1976–1977*, ed. David P. Chandler, Ben Kiernan, and Chanthou Boua. New Haven, CT: Yale University Southeast Asian Studies, 1988. Copyright © 1988 by Yale University Southeast Asian Studies. All rights reserved. Reproduced by permission.

Pol Pot (left) leads Cambodian guerrillas in the jungle in June 1979, after the Khmer Rouge were driven out of power. © AP Images.

accomplished them to the maximum, surpassing expectations, leaping forward.

All the exploiting classes who had previously been beaten down were beaten and cut down even further in 1976. They have declined. They are unable to rise again in the countryside, the cities, the offices, the revolutionary ranks, or in the Party. Now this beating down and this uprooting are not directed at one or two aspects of this problem. Instead, they represent an all-out attack on every aspect, digging down to unearth the roots of the exploiting classes, large or small.

As for individualism, whether of feudalists, capitalists, or of other classes not particularly poor, such as independent farmers, independent workers, and independent manual laborers, we have dug down and uprooted even more of this in 1976. We won't allow individualism to rise again.

We have also fought against individual privilege, impressively and profoundly in 1976. We have fought it in the Party, among the people, and in the revolutionary ranks.

These are the three aspects which reveal our victory in the task of waging a continuous social revolution. In 1976, we have done everything possible in national society and in our own ranks. We have transformed attitudes as well as the economy, culture, social welfare, technology, and education. We have mounted an all-out attack. Looking at the results, we see that we have been utterly victorious. On the surface, it's as if nothing has changed. But if we examine the essence of the struggle and class contradictions at every level of our socialist revolution, it's clear that we have seeped into every corner.

What emerges [from our scrutiny] are the good results of the entire Party. These spring from being united, boldly and steadily struggling with enemies who have intruded into the Party. The influence of our army is becoming clearer, as it increasingly becomes the authoritative instrument of the Party. If we hadn't made a deep and thorough socialist revolution in this fashion, the army would not be as pure or as united with the Party [as it is], and might run into obstacles.

A powerful force has entered the people, leading them to purify themselves, continuously driving out bad elements, making our national socialism ever more pure among the people, safeguarding the work of building socialism and defending the country.

Purifying Society

If our socialist revolution didn't seep into every corner, the Party, the army, the people, the offices and ministries will become confused, the 1976 Plan will be defeated, and so will the task of defending the country. Difficulties within the country and outside it are long-standing problems for the future.

This reveals important characteristics of the socialist revolution. The socialist revolution encompasses everything. This is what is basic about our revolution. The task of building socialism is not the basis; the task of defending the country is not the basis either. To be sure, building socialism and defending the country are important factors, but they stand on the socialist revolution itself, both for the immediate and the distant future.

In 1976, for example, speaking only of internal Party matters, while we are engaged in a socialist revolution, there is a sickness inside the Party, born in the time when we waged a people's and a democratic revolution. We cannot locate it precisely. The illness must emerge to be examined. Because the heat of the people's revolution and the heat of the democratic revolution were insufficient at the level of people's struggle and at the level of class struggle among all layers of the national democratic revolution, we search for the microbes within the Party without success. They are buried. As our socialist revolution advances, however, seeping more strongly into every corner of the Party, the army and among the people, we can locate the ugly microbes. They will be pushed out by the true nature of socialist revolution. We are encouraged to expel treacherous elements that pose problems to the Party and to our revolution. If we wait any longer, the microbes can do real damage. Thus we have characterized the socialist revolution. We should emphasize that the socialist revolution does not make any additional contradictions. Now there may be some people who think that the socialist revolution is too deep and too extensive, and gives birth to additional contradiction. But then these elements believe that class struggles are unnecessary to reveal contradictions. Contradictions exist. If we scratch the ground to bury them, they will rot us from within. They will rot society, rot the Party, and rot the army. If we don't wage a deep, extensive socialist revolution, these contradictions will increase in strength. To give an example: the string of traitors that we smashed recently had been organized secretly during the people's revolution and the democratic revolution. In those days, that sort of people could be alongside us. In a socialist era, they must be

The Wars in Indochina

The Cambodian genocide took place within the context of a long period of upheaval in the region as local peoples in Cambodia, Laos, and Vietnam tried to carve modern nation states out of what had been the French colony of Indochina.

In the first of these conflicts, the First Indochina War from 1946 to 1954, Vietnamese independence fighters fought France, which was seeking to regain control after World War II. Cambodia stayed out of the war, which ended in a fairly decisive victory for the Vietnamese. Afterward Indochina was divided into the states of Cambodia, Laos, North Vietnam, and South Vietnam.

North Vietnam was under Communist control, while South Vietnam was a democratic nation supported by the West. The separation of Vietnam resulted in a new series of conflicts in which the United States played a major part. In 1959, North Vietnamese Communists began to try to reunite the country, mostly using local insurgents in the south. To keep the south free of communism, the United States sent first military advisors then, beginning in 1965, regular combat troops. The Vietnam War lasted from 1965 until 1975 when, despite a massive US effort, neither they nor South Vietnamese forces were able to prevent a complete Communist takeover and reunification of the country. For much of the same period US interests participated in a "secret war" in Laos, trying and

cast aside. Now 1976 was a year of furious, diligent class struggle inside our Party. Many microbes emerged. Many networks came into view.

It's not true that we make revolution so as to produce contradictions. Contradictions have existed for a very long time. They were buried. We must expose them and the mistakes that have been made at certain levels. No Ministry of Health will discover them. The socialist revolution will discover them, as it seeps into the Party, the army, and the people, distinguishing between good and bad characteristics.

ultimately failing to prevent a Communist takeover there.

Cambodian leaders resented US involvement in Vietnam, and leader King Sihanouk allowed the Vietnamese Communists to use the port of Sihanoukville as well as border areas. US forces began to bomb those border areas, and in 1970 the ground war spilled over the border into Cambodia. That same year, Sihanouk was ousted by the US-supported General Lon Nol.

The result was a Cambodia roiled by conflict from 1970 to 1975, when as many as a half-million people died. Lon Nol's government forces, supported and supplied by the United States, fought against an awkward combination of supporters of Sihanouk, the North Vietnamese who occupied much of the country, and the rising movement known as the Khmer Rouge, which pledged to bring the exploitation of Cambodia to an end.

Despite temporary cooperation among Communist factions in the early 1970s, the Cambodians and Vietnamese have a mutual dislike that goes back centuries. These hatreds re-emerged during the years of the Cambodian genocide from 1975 to 1979. Numerous border conflicts and other disputes inspired Vietnam to launch an invasion in late 1978 and, within weeks, Vietnamese forces ousted the Khmer Rouge government. Although the Vietnamese continued to prop up a government in Phnom Penh made up of Cambodian loyalists, warfare continued in the countryside between the Vietnamese and remnants of the Khmer Rouge. The conflict lasted until the last Vietnamese forces left in 1989.

To make certain that our revolution will be steadfast, we need only to rely on our socialist revolution. We can't yet be certain if we have revealed all the treacherous elements. But we have taken important steps in the Party, the army and the people to assure the victory of the socialist revolution at every level. It is a combined effort. Standing on co-operative efforts must be tempered by observations made at every location, base, and organization. Whichever of these is involved, the Party can be built successfully as long as the socialist revolution is complete; the country can also be successfully defended and successfully built; on the other hand, whatever base or organization we are dealing with, if the revolution is fought badly and the Party is built badly, the movement will not advance rapidly, and daily tasks will not be rapidly accomplished.

Opposition Must Be Rooted Out

Sometimes there is no active opposition; there is only silence. Sometimes opposition emerges as confusion, breaking down our solidarity. If a socialist revolution is waged properly, problems [like these] are swiftly solved.

To sum up: this year we have waged a profound socialist revolution. We have also expelled the hidden, buried traitors from within the Party, the army, and the people. We can successfully defend and build the country now. Our socialist revolution has been the unifying theme of 1976. In 1973, we took care of the aspect of co-operatives. Before [1976], however, we weren't able to extend the revolution to the whole society, the entire Party, or the entire army. We have only been able to do so in 1976; we have done it very quickly. We have defended the country well. We haven't been confused; the process has not been long or exhausting. We have built the country well. But one year can't serve as the basis. Not everything has been accomplished. We must advance further in 1977 and later years. . . .

In the task of building socialism, we have already been victorious. We have expanded collectivism throughout society, throughout the co-operatives and in the countryside. We have had far better results than in 1975. Our collectives have all advanced in scope. Our villages are all collective. In addition, a certain number of towns have been collectivized. Wherever this has taken place, advances have been made.

In the cities, all the workers have become collectivized. So are the cooperative. This collectivism isn't of an ordinary kind, but of a higher variety. Methods of production are to be collectivized. Supplies and raw materials will be collectivized; work will be collectivized, and so on. This is not ordinary collectivism. It has a movable scenario, dividing forces that are sharp, those that are primary, from those that are secondary, those in front from those behind, and also in terms of quotas.

The rejection of old relations of production is the basis and the totality as well. Collective relations of production are expanding. Tasks are assigned to front-line units and to rear-echelon units, so as to build the country. In 1976, we lacked food, medicine, and supplies, but the strength of our collective organization was mighty. There were forces to deal blows in the front and forces to the rear. We could strike mighty blows. Provisions have now increased. As for the problem of water, we will dig connecting streams and canals and erect dikes in line with the provisions of the Plan. This is a dividend of pure collectivism, whose nature stems from our socialist revolution. There are several aspects—economic, cultural, social, technical and educational. In 1976, political consciousness has been of considerable importance in the army, in the Party, and among the people. *However, in comparative terms, political consciousness lags behind the other aspects.* It has not yet transformed the collectivity, even in economic terms.

At the level of the economy, the Party and the army have solved this issue, and at the level of livelihood they have had many successes. But the acceleration of consciousness lags behind the pace of collectivization. If we examine all aspects of collectivizations in 1976, we can see that *the crucial problems are the problem of the Party and the problem of cadre* [party officials]. To solve problems of collectivization in the Party, each level must be good, spreading its influence into the army and among the people to make them good as well. Progress in collectivization in 1976 has been due to the Party. What has been slow, in terms of consciousness, also comes from the Party, which lags behind in this regard. In the future, the biggest problem will be to increase collectivization at every level of the Party and in every aspect of the economy and people's consciousness within the Party, to make it ever more efficacious. Do what you can to make people welcome this policy, which is certainly correct. The arrangements for implementing the policy are correct also. We need to struggle, however, to build up internal aspects, so they can be understood and clear, and so people can understand the reasons for our policies. Waging a socialist revolution provides its own rationale. Individualism and individual methods must be driven out. So must individual conduct. At that point the people can understand the rationale. In the future we must put our trust in revolutionary awareness and in socialism as they exist inside the Party. The Party's line has emerged from its particular movement, which is very fast. Political work and political consciousness must also be fast, so as to reveal to the people the benefits of collectivism with clear examples from every type of organization.

Cambodian Women in the Revolutionary War for People's National Liberation (1973)

Khmer Rouge Wartime Propaganda

The following viewpoint is a piece of propaganda emphasizing the role of Cambodian women in defeating the imperialism of the United States, which was then involved in the Vietnam War that had spread into Cambodia. The viewpoint notes how women took part in both combat as well as in support roles, and how a number of women made sacrifices such as leaving behind their children in order to serve the revolution. It also presents a story of how a group of female guerilla fighters were able to trick enemy fighters during a village celebration. The viewpoint is excerpted from a collection of documents compiled and translated by scholars in the Cambodian Genocide Program at Yale University.

Just like the men, Cambodian women, yesterday and today, have contributed greatly to the struggle against foreign aggression in defense of the fatherland.

After the anti-national and anti-popular coup d'état [overthrow of the government] on March 18, 1970, the group of traitors Lon Nol, Sirik Matak, and Son Ngoc Thanh [then government leaders] sold Cambodia cheap to the U.S. imperialists and allowed them to transform it into a neo-colony and a military base.

Since then, with the loss of its independence, neutrality, sovereignty and territorial integrity, Cambodia has been plunged into a most cruel war which brings untold suffering to the women and people of the country.

Applying the [US president Richard] Nixon doctrine which consists of making Indochinese fight Indochinese and Cambodians fight Cambodians, the American imperialists, their lackeys in Saigon [South Vietnam] and Bangkok [Thailand], and the group of traitors in Phnom Penh, have perpetrated innumerable crimes against our people.

Implementing the policy of "kill all, burn all, destroy all," everywhere the U.S. puppet troops go, they sow mourning, misery and desolation. The enemy every day commits mass slaughter in which neither individuals nor bonzes (Buddhist monks) nor priests are spared, in their pillage and rape that the Phnom Penh press and world opinion have convincingly revealed. Every day their planes pour millions of tons of bombs on our territory, killing men, women, old and young indiscriminately, devastating and systematically flattening the houses and rice fields of the peaceful populations, as well as historic monuments such as Angkor Wat, and monasteries.

In the areas provisionally controlled by the enemy, apart from fascist repression, women are still obliged to cope with the high cost of living, a lack of necessary elementary provisions, notably rice, and find it very difficult to make ends meet. To this are added other worries: their husbands and their sons could be conscripted at any moment at all, their daughters kidnapped and raped by the troops of Phnom Penh and Saigon. The American way of life, a depraved society, and prostitution have poisoned the minds of so many girls and women.

More than ever, Cambodian women know that the only possible way to free themselves from this thrall-ring is to join in the struggle with the men, without hesitation or compromise, against the American aggressors and their valets for the national liberation.

Women's Contributions

At the front, women take part in combat, in medical teams, in destroying all communications, in voluntary work teams. Behind the lines, women play a top-level role. Numerous guerrilla units have been formed entirely of women. Women take charge of various tasks, replacing men who have left for the front: village defense, making booby-traps, agricultural production, planting, medical work, etc. . . . Mothers have shared their children's meals with fighters from FAPLNK (Cambodian People's National Liberation Armed Forces), others have entrusted their young ones to neighbors, in order to fulfill liaison missions.

Many other such examples demonstrate the political responsibility of women in Cambodia. While carrying out their national duty, the women of Cambodia are also well aware of their international obligations. The primordial task which lies before them is to stand in the front line against imperialism, particularly U.S. imperialism. In this, they are offering their worthy contribution to the cause of popular national liberation of the peoples of the world, notably those of Asia, Africa and Latin America, which are not yet free of the yoke of colonialism, both old and new.

Moreover, women in Cambodia possess a legitimate pride in having helped to improve the conditions of women in general. For, arming themselves with their high revolutionary morality and demonstrating supreme revolutionary heroism, they have achieved exploits which our people hold in high esteem. They are thus contributing to tearing apart those backward perceptions of women which still have currency in the world.

"All our sisters," writes Madame Khieu Ponnary, President of the Association of Democratic Women of Kampuchea [Cambodia], "are determined to lead their just struggle against American imperialism and its puppets, until final victory under the direction of the National United Front of Kampuchea, with the

Head of State, Prince Norodom Sihanouk, as president. In this just fight of ours for the ideals of independence, peace, liberty, and progress, we know that we are not alone. From all over the world we receive messages of solidarity. Demonstrations of support are breaking out in all parts of the globe in aid of the just cause of the Cambodian people, and condemning unequivocally the crimes of American imperialism and its valets. May we now take this opportunity to express the deep gratitude of the Association of Democratic Women of Kampuchea to the women of the whole world, without forgetting American women, who, faithful to the same ideals of peace, justice, liberty and progress have spontaneously taken their stand by our side. They have in this way contributed to isolate American imperialism and its valets, and to bring about the triumph of the just cause of the forces for independence, democracy and peace in the world."

Young Women Guerilla Fighters Overrun an Enemy Post

Village T is situated on the edges of the area provisionally controlled by the enemy in Kompong Speu province. A company of puppet troops set up a position there under the orders of their torturer-captain. Since then, the villagers had to cope with all sorts of trials and exactions. For even the shortest journey, they have to seek permission from the commander of the post. Otherwise they would wind up accused of being agents of the "Khmer Rouges" or the "Vietcong—North Vietnamese" and would be subjected to the worst sorts of torture. Many have come out of such treatment sick, others have gone mad or even died. The families of the prisoners, in order to get their loved ones free, often had to sell what little they had (house, plot of land, buffalo) and even their own children to pay the torturer-captain the ransom demanded. The villagers must still pay "loans" in the form of money, rice, pork, poultry, which no one dares try to avoid. Worse still, the traitorous captain and his men embark on orgies of rape against the girls and the women of the village.

A female Khmer Rouge fighter carries an assault rifle in the jungle of western Cambodia in 1981. The Khmer Rouge encouraged women to serve as fighters in the revolution. © Alex Bowie/Hulton Archive/Getty Images.

The inhabitants of this area, victims of exploitation and sorts of robbery by the torturer-captain and his men, have a miserable life full of humiliation. However, despite severe enemy repression day and night, the local branch of FUNK (National United Front of Kampuchea) is still intact, to guide the people in their struggle.

In order to free the villagers from the cruel claws of the eager puppets of the American imperialist aggressor, the local branch of the FUNK decided to wipe out the enemy position without endangering the population, in conformity with its wishes.

Representatives of the FUNK branches from surrounding villages met secretly to set in motion a plan to attack the position. One question raised, however, stopped everyone short: "How can we attack the enemy if none of us, even the guerrillas, are armed, because of the continual troops' searches of the houses and sweeps into the forest?" When a lively discussion of how to find a solution began, a young girl guerrilla interrupted: "We must take the enemy's arms in order to wipe him out."

"An excellent idea," everyone nodded. "But how are we going to do it?" they asked. "None of us can even approach the enemy position. How, then, could we possibly get inside?"

The young girl, with a childish smile on her lips, started explaining in detail how her group intended to outwit the enemy. Everyone approved of her well thought-out plan.

A week passed. The carnival atmosphere in village T was quite out of the ordinary. Here, they were putting up a lean-to; there, a kitchen. Over there, they piled up the rice; over there they cut down trees and plants for the decorations. On that day the people from the neighboring villages came to village T in large numbers, some bringing poultry with them, some bringing vegetables. Festival music could be heard from one end of the village to the other. It seemed that a wedding was about to take place.

A Clever Deception

In the barracks, the soldiers also arranged the tables for a feast. Nothing unusual about that; the parents of the bride and bridegroom had come to the quarters to ask the captain's permission for their children to get married. Permission was granted on condition that the parents organize a feast that same day for him and his men. "But," he added, "I want to be served by the bride herself and all the bridesmaids will wait on my men. None of the others will be allowed into the barracks today." The parents reluctantly decided to give in to the wishes of the traitor.

Three o'clock in the afternoon; twenty people, young and old, men and women, headed towards the barracks, carrying on their heads or on their shoulders the provisions for the feast.

When they arrived in front of the post, the sentry stopped them, and told them to put down their loads. He called to other troops inside and they came out to carry in the provisions. Then the sentry ordered our people to go back to the village immediately.

Four-thirty: Ten girls elegantly dressed and accompanied by hefty boys carrying five cases of alcohol, presented themselves at the post. This time, the sentry let the girls in, but stood in the way of the men and ordered them to go back home.

At the sight of the lovely ladies, four plain-clothes officers drinking at a table rejoiced.

One of them asked the girls:

"You, girls, can you dance the *ramvong* [a refined dance for celebration]?"

"Yes, of course we can," they replied.

This set the four shouting and clapping their hands excitedly.

Then, the captain gave the order to three of the soldiers to stand guard, one at the entrance and the two others at the lookout, while he told the rest to relax at the tables with their rifles by their side, taking turns to do guard duty.

Hearing this order, the girls begged the commander:

"We are afraid of guns. Monsieur le Capitaine, please don't let your men sit down or dance with us with all those rifles! Otherwise how can we generously give you our attention and our dancing?"

At this, laughter filled the room. The officers wanted to appear gallant.

"My darlings, you have nothing to fear from these rifles. We would never use them on girls so lovely and fresh as you all are right now! If we don't carry our guns, how can we defend you when the Khmers Krahom come?" (Khmers Krahom is the popular Cambodian term for Khmer Rouges, or Khmer Reds.)

"Yes," replied the prettiest one, "we agree with you, but we only want you to put your rifles in some place where they won't get in the way when we're dancing."

The captain granted the girls' request and told his men to put their rifles in bundles near the tables.

Then the party started. First the meal was served. The three prettiest girls waited on the officers, the others on the soldiers. They concentrated on being attentive and thought only of one thing: to make them drink as much as possible.

The bell went for the changing of the guard but not one of the merrymaking soldiers took the least notice. They kept on drinking glass after glass and quickly got drunker and drunker. The three angry soldiers on guard came in and sat down at the tables cleared for them by our girls.

The drunken soldiers and officers all shouted and sang loudly. They forgot about dancing. All of a sudden, one of the girls clapped her hands three times.

Quick as a flash, without giving the enemy time to work out what was happening, the girls firmly grabbed the guns and pointed them at the soldiers.

Simultaneously, one girl fired a shot and ordered the soldiers "Hands up!" They were caught off guard and in no time ten hefty youths, the same ones who had carried the casks of alcohol, charged into the room and tied up the soldiers.

The villagers from round about heard the shots and ran towards the post to find out what had happened. An unexpected but welcome sight met their eyes. They gathered for a meeting in the fields to denounce the crimes committed by the torturer-captain and his whole board, straw dogs for the traitors of Phnom Penh and eager servants of U.S. imperialism.

That same night, the guerrillas marched the captive soldiers into the liberated zone and presented them to the local FUNK headquarters.

Village T as well as the surrounding villages were thus liberated and their inhabitants became masters of their lands, their villages and their communes, and they benefited from their newly-won democratic freedoms.

Blue Scarves and Yellow Stars: Classification and Symbolization in the Cambodian Genocide

Gregory H. Stanton

In the following viewpoint, a scholar examines the motivations be-hind the Cambodian genocide, which resulted in the deaths of as many as two million people. He notes that Khmer Rouge leaders adopted a radical form of communism advocated by twentieth cen-tury leaders such as Vladimir Lenin, the guiding force of Russia's revolution beginning in 1917, and Mao Tse-Tung, the Communist leader of China from 1949 to 1976. Khmer Rouge leaders went to great lengths to classify groups of enemies of the revolution who had to be eliminated. These undesirables included urbanites, Buddhist monks, ethnic minorities, and those deemed to be under Vietnamese influence. Gregory H. Stanton is a research professor in genocide studies and prevention at George Mason University and founder of the organization Genocide Watch.

April 17, 1975 was a day of hope and horror for the people of Cambodia. It was the day the Khmer Rouge Communists rolled into Phnom Penh and took control of the government. Cheering people lined the streets hoping for peace. What they got instead was horror—one of the worst genocides in human history.

Premeditated murder. Genocide as state policy. Intentional killing of all "class enemies," elimination of cities and city dwellers, destruction of every ethnic and religious minority, mass murder of the Eastern Zone of Democratic Kampuchea, execution of all teachers, doctors, lawyers, soldiers and government officials. If you wore glasses, or could speak a foreign language, or were educated, you were classified as an enemy; were arrested, tortured, then killed. From 1975 through 1978, according to censuses taken by the Cambodian Genocide Project in Cambodian villages, 1.7 million to 2.2 million people died out of a population of eight million. Half a million to a million were intentionally murdered. Another million were starved or worked to death in the forced labor communes the Khmer Rouge imposed at gunpoint in every region of the country.

The horror began even before April 17, 1975, in regions controlled by the Khmer Rouge. People who lived in Prey Veng, Svay Rieng, Takeo, and other provinces that fell in 1972 tell of the mass murders that began in those provinces even then.

The blue-print for the Khmer Rouge revolution, the *Mein Kampf* of Kampuchea, was written in 1956 by Khieu Samphan, in his Ph.D. dissertation in economics at a French university. Khieu Samphan and his close friends, Pol Pot (a.k.a. Saloth Sar) and Ieng Sary were all members of the French Communist party while they were students in France. It was and is a Marxist-Leninist party. It was also Stalinist. The Khmer Rouge leaders read the Marxist theorists of the day, people like Jean-Paul Sartre, André Gunder Frank, and Mao-Tse-tung. And they planned a Communist revolution to put their ideas into practice. Later, when the Maoist Cultural Revolution wreaked terror in China, they wholeheartedly added its radical equalitarianism to their own.

Marxism-Leninism (and its Maoist variant) teaches that revolutions must be violent, that class struggles are inevitable, and that class enemies must be crushed. In every Communist revolution so far, crushed means killed.

Apologists for Communist revolutions like to use euphemisms like purged, eliminated, or liquidated. Euphemisms allow people to avoid thinking; they are shields against consciousness; earplugs to shut out the screams of the murdered and the cries of the conscience. I will not use euphemisms here. In Democratic Kampuchea, the Khmer Rouge murdered about two million people.

In this [viewpoint] I will begin to explain why and how the Pol Pot regime committed this genocide. I have spent much of the past eight years working to bring the Khmer Rouge leaders to justice for their crimes. I will describe what interviews with survivors inside Cambodia have revealed about the first two operations in the genocidal process: classification and symbolization.

Classification and Symbolization

At the beginning of their planning for the Holocaust, the National Socialists in Germany passed detailed laws defining membership in the Jewish race, and then conducted inquiries to identify who were members of the race. Later, they decreed that each Jew had to wear a yellow star. It was a symbolic marker. It signified that this person was not to be seen as an individual person but as a member of a class, a classification determined by religion and "race." The yellow star marked a classification of people the Nazis had decided to kill. The ultimate depersonalization—murder, killing persons—was preceded by the depersonalization of classification and symbolization, the Nuremberg laws and the yellow star.

The Khmer Rouge classified, too. First they classified people as "base people"—people under Khmer Rouge control before April 17, 1975—and new people—mostly city people. They had read André Gunder Frank's Marxist theory that cities are parasitic on the countryside, that only labor value is true value, that cities extract surplus value from the rural areas. Therefore immediately after they took power, the Khmer Rouge evacuated all the cities at gunpoint. Patients in hospitals in the middle of operations were forced to leave, and to die. Women in labor were made to get up and walk and their new babies died in the scorching sun. A whole infant ward at the Calmette Hospital was abandoned when the Khmer Rouge forced the staff to leave. The ward became a mass grave.

The new people were marked for heavier labor, less food, and much harsher treatment than the base people. Children were taken away from their parents and forced to work in children's brigades. If a new person complained of the food shortages and slave labor, he or she was taken away to the killing fields.

In 1976 people were reclassified as full rights (base) people, candidates, and depositees—so called because they included most of the new people who had been deposited from the cities into the communes. Depositees were marked for destruction. Their rations were reduced to two bowls of rice soup per day. Hundreds of thousands starved.

The Khmer Rouge leadership boasted over their radio station that only one or two million people out of the population were needed to build the new agrarian communist utopia. As for the others, as their proverb put it, "if they survive no gain, if they die, no loss."

Hundreds of thousands of the new people, and later the depositees, were taken out, shackled, to dig their own mass graves. Then the Khmer Rouge soldiers beat them to death with iron bars and hoes or buried them alive. A Khmer Rouge extermination prison directive ordered, "Bullets are not to be wasted."

The Khmer Rouge also classified by religion and ethnic group. They abolished all religion and dispersed minority groups, forbidding them to speak their languages or to practice their customs.

The Cham Muslims were especially singled out for murder. A Central Committee directive ordered, "The Cham nation no longer exists on Kampuchean soil belonging to the Khmer. Accordingly the Cham nationality, language, customs and reli-

Holding a pistol, a Khmer Rouge soldier orders shop owners to abandon their shops in Phnom Penh, Cambodia, on April 17, 1975. A large portion of the city's dwellers were forced to evacuate. © AP Images/Christoph Froehder.

gious beliefs must be immediately abolished. Those who fail to obey this order will suffer all the consequences for their acts of opposition to Angkar," the Khmer Rouge high command.

Whole Cham villages were murdered. Cham children were taken away from their parents and raised as Khmers. Chams were not permitted to speak their language. Though Muslims, they were forced to eat pork. Their leaders were killed. "We drank tears," said a Cham to me.

Most Chams were classified as "new people" because they were Cham. Censuses I have taken in Cham villages show that a quarter to a third, over a hundred thousand of them, died out of a pre-Khmer Rouge population of about 200,000. There is evidence that the Khmer Rouge planned to kill the rest of the Cham and were only stopped by the Vietnamese invasion on Christmas Day of 1978.

The Khmer Rouge also disrobed all Buddhist monks, subjected them to brutal forced labor and wiped out the practice of

Buddhism. They did the same to Christianity, leaving only one Khmer pastor, who survived only because he hid his identity. Chinese and Vietnamese minorities were also marked for murder.

Perhaps the most massive murder of all was committed on the population of the Eastern zone of Democratic Kampuchea in 1978, in the provinces of Svay Rieng, Prey Veng and parts of Kandal and Kompong Cham near the Vietnamese border. The Khmer Rouge leaders declared the entire population of this region to have "Khmer bodies, but Vietnamese heads." In 1978 most of the Eastern zone people were evacuated to other provinces where they were placed in forced labor communes, then systematically underfed and overworked, often to death. Many were murdered outright.

In December, 1986, while interviewing witnesses in that region with Australian historian Ben Kiernan, we made a dramatic discovery of the symbolic means the Khmer Rouge leaders used to mark Eastern zone people for extermination. It is the clinching proof that the Eastern zone genocide was ordered by the Khmer Rouge leadership in Phnom Penh.

The people of the Eastern zone were evacuated up the rivers and roads to Phnom Penh, then sent onward to other provinces. *At Phnom Penh, the Khmer Rouge issued every man, woman and child from the Eastern zone a new blue and white checked scarf, a kroma.* The Khmer Rouge then required them to wear the scarf at all times. "Other people wore red and white or yellow and white scarves, but weren't allowed to wear blue and white scarves," Huy Rady, an eye witness explained. "People from the Eastern zone would be known by their scarf. If you were wearing a blue scarf they would kill you. There was a plan to kill all the Eastern zone people. They were not going to spare any of them."

The blue scarf was the yellow star. It was a symbol of a classification made by the Khmer Rouge Central Committee and imposed by its own cadres in Phnom Penh. It is the clearest evidence we have yet gathered of the genocidal intent of the Khmer Rouge. As a witness told me, "I have seen the Khmer Rouge come to a place and take away the people with blue scarves. Every day was a killing day. They put on a killing sign."

Chhun Vun of lower Neak Leung village explained, "They could tell who was an Eastern zone person. No one else wore blue scarves. The blue scarves were distributed to us directly by Pol Pot's Standing Group, the Permanent Committee of the Party. They distributed them to everyone of the Eastern Zone. The scarves were distributed as a sign in Phnom Penh city at Chbar Ampeou."

I asked Chhun Vun, "If a Pursat base person wanted to wear a blue scarf would the Khmer Rouge permit it?" He answered, "They were absolutely not allowed to wear the clothes of the Eastern Zone people. They planned to kill us all."

Genocide

It is human to classify. Indeed, structural linguists who follow Roman Jakobson believe that classification and combination are the two fundamental operations of the human mind. We classify whenever we name something or describe someone. Human beings are the symbol-using animal; in symbolizing, we classify. But our symbols and our classifications are made, are invented, by us. They are our product. They are abstractions away from the concrete reality of the world of persons.

The problem is not that we humans classify. It is that we treat the classifications as if they had ultimate reality. We forget that it is we who made the classifications and we treat our abstractions as if they were concrete. To use Whitehead's term, we misplace concreteness. We human beings overvalue our abstractions and turn them against other persons and even against ourselves. Like the nuclear weapons and guns we have invented because of our extraordinary ability to symbolize, we turn our own creations, our own symbolic classifications, against ourselves. And we kill with them.

Classifications and symbolizations that define group boundaries and that exclude people who are enemies are by nature depersonalizing. Totalitarian regimes like the Khmer Rouge are regimes of ultimate depersonalization. Even the leaders referred to themselves as Brother Number One and Brother Number Two in their orders to the Director of the Tuol Sleng extermination prison.

Genocide is defined in the international convention for the Prevention and Punishment of the Crime of Genocide, as "the intentional destruction in whole or in part of a national, ethnical, racial or religious group, as such."

The Khmer Rouge committed genocide when they classified the Cham Muslims, the Buddhist monks, Christians, and other groups as class enemies and then destroyed them. They may also have committed legal genocide, and certainly committed politicide, a crime against humanity, by classifying part of the Democratic Kampuchean national group, the people of the Eastern Zone, as enemies, marking them with blue scarves, and marching them to their deaths.

Classification and symbolization are the first two operations in the genocidal process. Later operations, which may be both concurrent and sequential, are vilification, preparation, and extermination.

Vilification (dehumanization), the third stage of genocide, is the process by which members of a class are designated as enemies. The Nazis vilified Jews as subhuman rats and vermin. In the Tuol Sleng extermination prison, people—persons—were photographed with numbers and forced to "confess" they were animals, not persons, before being murdered by the guards. People of the Eastern Zone were vilified as possessing corrupt, enemy Vietnamese minds.

Preparation, the penultimate stage of genocide, is the operation when extermination prisons are built and members of vilified groups (class enemies, the Cham, people from the Eastern zone) are transported to them. It is the moment when Dr. Mengele, the Doctor of Death, beckons to those who are doomed.

One of the striking needs of the genocidal mind is the need for orderly determination of who will be included in the groups to be killed. The Nazis kept meticulous records of their crimes, including records of those classified and identified for murder, the lists of the damned. The Khmer Rouge, too, kept voluminous records in their extermination prisons, and tortured their victims to reveal names of others in the network of class enemies. They photographed each victim of the Tuol Sleng prison, including the children. Kinship identification was enough for condemnation to death, since it was Khmer Rouge policy to kill entire families. The stated purpose was to prevent later bitterness toward the Angkar by the children of enemies who had been executed.

The final criminal act of genocide is extermination. The individuals identified as members of vilified groups are taken to the killing fields and murdered. At this stage a strange means rationality takes over, an ethic of efficiency. The most efficient, lowest cost method of mass murder is preferred and bureaucracies are organized to administer the murder in an orderly, "rational" way. The SS chose an ordinary insecticide, Zyklon B, as the lowest cost, most efficient means of exterminating the Jewish "vermin". The Khmer Rouge murder weapons of choice were ordinary hoes and iron bars. The victims were tied together in a line, and forced to kneel at the edge of mass graves they had been forced to dig. Then the Khmer Rouge guards beat each victim to death by blows to the skull, severing the spinal cord. In Kandal and Kompong Speu provinces, along with the many mass graves filled with thousands of bodies (Choeng Ek—8000, Tonle Bati—4000, etc.), there are unfilled mass graves prepared for thousands of additional victims. The planning necessary to efficiently dispose of bodies requires a pathological order, a bureaucracy of death. As Max Weber pointed out, even the most irrational end can be pursued by rational means.

The ends justifies the means mentality of Marxism-Leninism and of all other totalitarian ideologies is what makes them so radically evil. Kierkegaard's "teleological suspension of the ethical" is taken to its extreme. In the name of creating a perfect new world, all morality is suspended, all persons are merely means to the end. Class enemies are to be killed.

Genocide is the pattern of human history, not its aberration. More people have died from genocides in this century than from all the wars combined. There are many types of genocides. Many of them are national, ethnical, racial, or religious like those committed against the Jews, the Native Americans, the Armenians, the Bengalis in Bangladesh/East Pakistan, the Hutu in Burundi, and countless others. But the most massive genocides of our century have been part of politicides committed by totalitarian regimes, by National Socialists and Marxist-Leninists. Two million murdered in Cambodia. Three million intentionally starved to death in the Ukraine. Sixty million murdered in the Soviet Union. Twenty-five million murdered under Mao. In those regimes the genocidal process has been glorified by ideology, by the Nazi doctrine of the master race and the Aryan nation, by the Marxist-Leninist doctrine of class enemies and communism.

For the future of mankind, anthropologists must make the study, the understanding, and the conquest of genocide a central goal of our vocation. Our understanding of the processes of classification and symbolization will be a key to attacking genocide yet to come, to preventing genocide, the scourge of humanity.

A Former Cambodian High School Became a Torture and Killing Center

CJ

One of the most vivid surviving reminders of the Cambodian genocide is Tuol Sleng, or Security Prison 21 (S-21). It is a former high school in Phnom Penh, Cambodia's capital, which local Khmer Rouge officials used as a torture center. The site remains in place, with some reconstruction, as both a memorial and destination for tourists. In the following viewpoint, a journalist describes S-21 and a list of ten posted rules describing how inmates were to behave. While many died at S-21, others who were tortured there were eventually taken to the killing field of Choeung Ek, outside Phnom Penh, to be murdered. That site, where as many as seventeen thousand were killed, remains as a memorial. CJ is a writer for the Tokyo Reporter, *an English-language newspaper in Japan.*

It is estimated that during the Cambodian Genocide (1975–1979) 1.7 million people lost their lives at the hands of the Khmer Rouge. During that time, radical left-wing politics mixed with a complete lack of regard for human life to create one of the most vicious and despicable reigns of terror in the history of man.

Teachers, professors, farmers, engineers, students and skilled artisans were murdered. Entire populations of cities were either starved or forced out from their homes into collective farms.

Those who were deemed to be in opposition, or considered as posing a potential threat, to the Khmer Rouge Government (or Angkar) were brought to Tuol Sleng (also known as S-21, or "Security Office 21"), a former high school converted to a prison, in Phnom Penh. Here, amid what can only be described as pure madness, 14,000 prisoners were interrogated, tortured, beaten, and "exterminated."

Over the years since, the crimes of the Khmer Rouge during the Cambodian Genocide went mostly undocumented. Today, Tuol Sleng is a museum dedicated to those that might have otherwise been forgotten.

The Ten Rules of Tuol Sleng

For prisoners at Tuol Sleng, a typical day consisted of nothing short of sheer horror and the strict adherence to ten rules . . .

1. You must answer accordingly to my questions. Do not turn them away.

There are four main buildings (A, B, C, and D) set in approximately a horseshoe shape around an open central yard of grass and trees. Only the first floors of all the buildings are open for viewing.

A large iron fence, topped with barbed wire, surrounds the entire 600-meter by 400-meter compound. Land-mine victims ask for change at the gated entrance off Street 113, bordering the property.

2. Do not try to hide the facts by making pretexts of this and that. You are strictly prohibited to contest me.

The first floor of Building A has ten open cells (formerly classrooms) extending down a hallway that runs at the edge of the greenery. In the hallway, the walls are a washed mix of deteriorating white and gray concrete.

3. Do not be a fool for you are a chap who dares to thwart the revolution.

In each room, five three-foot iron bars, used for shackling prisoners, extend vertically from the alternating yellow and red tile floor near the entrance. Their ends are hooked at the top. The entrance door is wood and the windows have iron bars running horizontally and vertically. A single bed frame sits in the middle of the room. Various clamps and other steel implements, used in the torture and shackling procedure, rest on the bed. A large black and white photo displaying the torture of a prisoner hangs on the wall. A rusted US Army ammo box sits next to the implements, apparently used for their storage.

4. You must immediately answer my questions without wasting time to reflect.

Building B sits next to Building A and forms a right angle in the courtyard. At this junction there is a large wooden structure at the edge of the grass. It is composed of two vertical columns and one horizontal beam. The beam hangs roughly ten feet off the ground. Three eyelets, separated proportionately, hang down from the beam. A large cracked clay pot sits at its edge.

As depicted in a painting by Tuol Sleng survivor (one of the few) Vann Nath, selected prisoners were hoisted up through the eyelets with rope, turned upside down, and dunked headfirst into the clay pot—at the time filled with water—as a means of interrogation.

5. Do not tell me either about your immoralities or the revolution.

Building B houses a series of rooms. The majority of which feature photos of some of the prisoners: Cambodians, Vietnamese, Thais, Laotians, New Zealanders, Americans, men, women, and children. They are mostly front and side view mug shots. They are numbered and dated. Some necks have chains around them. Some hands look to be tucked behind backs. Some women hold babies. Some men and boys wear berets. All look very sad.

A Cambodian man walks past exhibits at the Tuol Sleng Genocide Museum in 2010. The photos depict the suffering prisoners endured there. © Paula Bronstein/Getty Images News/ Getty Images.

6. While getting lashes or electrification you must not cry at all.

Number 108 is a man with protruding eyes. Number 408 is a scared young girl. Number 275 is a gray-haired old woman. Number 189 is a man who is missing one of his arms. Number 66 is a man exhibiting a strong jaw but a very emaciated upper body. Numbers 12 and 17 are young boys.

7. Do nothing. Sit still and wait for my orders. If there is no order, keep quiet. When I ask you to do nothing, you must do it right away without protesting.

In the last room, shackling irons sit behind a glass case. Photos of the disposal areas for the bodies hang on the walls. In them, skulls line up in a field like melons at a market. Bones fill burial pits like kindling before the lighting of a fire. A concrete bust of Pol Pot sits chained to the floor. It was sculpted by one of the prisoners.

8. Do not make pretexts about Kampuchea Krom [a histori-cally Cambodian region in southern Vietnam] in order to hide your jaw of traitor.

Building C and Building B sit next to each other, end to end. An information sign indicates that on the third floor "the braid of barbed wires prevents the desperate victims from committing suicide."

A labyrinth of brick walls forms makeshift cells all along the bottom floor. Chains are attached to the individual cell floors. The horizontal dimensions of the cells are perhaps twice as big as the inside of a chimney.

9. If you do not follow all the above rules, you shall get many lashes of electric wire.

Building D forms a right angle with Building C to complete the horseshoe shape around the courtyard. Inside are actual torture devices. More paintings by Vann Nath hang above many devices to give a visual description of their grisly use.

Some procedures involved: shackling a prisoner face down in a coffin-like container filled to the brim with water, suspending a prisoner from the ceiling with rope and dunking him headfirst into a barrel of water, and pinning a prisoner to the floor while chemicals are poured over one of his immobilized hands gripped in a wrench.

10. If you disobey any point of my regulations you shall get either ten lashes or five shocks of electric discharge.

In the final room, skulls of former prisoners form a chalkboard-sized map of Cambodia. It is mounted on the wall and is the prominent feature of the room, and perhaps all of Tuol Sleng itself. The Mekong River flows in red between the skulls through the length of the country.

Forensic Investigations Reveal the Scale of Cambodia's Suffering

Craig Etcheson

In the years after the fall of the Khmer Rouge regime in 1979, its leaders have tried to either deny or minimize the mass killings. In the following viewpoint, a historian reports how investigation of Cambodia's many mass graves establishes firmly that genocide occurred from 1975 to 1979, the years of the Khmer Rouge's Democratic Kampuchea. He notes that many of the killing centers were located near the Khmer Rouge's security offices, and the majority of the victims abandoned there died in ways other than warfare, disease, or hunger. Eyewitness accounts, he claims, support these forensic investigations. Craig Etcheson is the author of After the Killing Fields: Lessons of the Cambodian Genocide *and has served as both a program director at Yale University's Cambodian Genocide Program and a visiting scholar at Johns Hopkins University.*

"They say that dead men tell no tales," but in fact they do. Many stories have been told by investigators unearthing mass graves in the Balkans, Central America, and elsewhere.

Information gathered from mass graves can help resolve disputes about the nature of communal or international conflict, and shed light on historical facts. With modern forensic science, mass graves yield evidence that can be used to prosecute war crimes and other violations of international humanitarian law. Mass graves may even help to relieve the anguish of families whose loved ones disappeared in a time of war. In Cambodia mass graves dating to Cambodia's 1975 to 1979 revolution have told all these tales, and more.

The Communist Party of Kampuchea, popularly known as the Khmer Rouge, led Cambodia's revolution. It was one of the most violent revolutions of the twentieth century. Demographers estimate that two million or more lives were lost in the four years that the Khmer Rouge ruled Cambodia, from a population of around seven million before the uprising. This scale of violence earned Cambodia a dubious title, the Killing Fields.

Thousands of Mass Graves

Between 1995 and 2003 researchers from the Documentation Center of Cambodia identified 19,471 mass graves at 348 sites located throughout the country. Investigators believe that these mass graves contained the remains of more than 1.1 million victims of execution. Virtually all these mass graves were located within 2 kilometers of what the Khmer Rouge euphemistically called security offices, but which might more accurately be labeled extermination centers. More than 185 such extermination centers have been discovered. At most of these sites witnesses have testified that the mass graves were created during the years the Khmer Rouge held power, and that the victims were detained in the so-called security offices prior to their execution. Although the Documentation Center's figures are only estimates, it is clear that whatever the actual numbers may be, they are large.

Senior Khmer Rouge officials have attempted to explain the existence of the mass graves by asserting that they were created by Vietnamese spies who had infiltrated the revolution. However,

An exhumed killing field in 1981 yielded the skeletons of executed Cambodians. Hundreds of mass graves like this one have been found. © David A. Harvey/National Geographic/Getty Images.

the uniform distribution of the mass graves throughout populated areas of the country casts doubt on this claim. More tellingly, senior Khmer Rouge officials are contradicted by many lower-level Khmer Rouge cadre [fighters or officials] who have testified that they carried out the executions at the mass grave sites on the orders of senior officials within the Khmer Rouge organization.

The vast number of mass graves in Cambodia, along with their uniform distribution, are in and of themselves legally probative facts. In order for acts such as murder to qualify as a crime against humanity, the acts must be mass and systematic. Some twenty thousand mass graves distributed relatively evenly across Cambodia clearly meet these criteria.

Forensic work at the Documentation Center of Cambodia has demonstrated that the individuals interred in the mass graves were not merely soldiers killed in combat nor victims of nonviolent causes of death such as disease or starvation. Many of the remains—bones of men, women, and children—exhibit evidence of trauma, including blunt force trauma, sharp force trauma, and gunshot wounds. This physical evidence confirms the testimony of former Khmer Rouge who have described in detail the methods they used to execute their victims.

The Cambodian People's Party (CPP) has ruled Cambodia since the 1979 overthrow of the Khmer Rouge regime. The CPP has systematically exploited the mass graves as a mechanism to aggregate political support ever since they came to power. Memorials created at many mass grave sites are the locations for annual national observances: the Day of Liberation on January 7th, marking the ouster of the Khmer Rouge regime, and the Day of Hatred on May 20th, intended to remind the population of their suffering under the Khmer Rouge, as well as the ruling party's claim that it delivered Cambodia's people from that suffering.

Cambodians Have Adopted New Rituals to Honor Genocide Victims

Many ordinary Cambodians have come to view the mass graves not as a focus of political activity, but rather as a locus for ancestor veneration. With some two million people missing and presumed dead after the Khmer Rouge regime, Cambodian traditions of ancestor veneration were severely challenged. Cambodians consequently adapted traditional ceremonies for paying respect to their dead, and commonly perform these rituals with the remains of anonymous victims at genocide memorials serving as a proxy for missing relatives.

In one variation of this practice, at Wat Skoun in Kampong Cham Province, a genocide memorial now contains only femurs and tibia exhumed from nearby mass graves. The crania were gradually [taken away] as religious officials permitted bereaved families to claim one exhumed skull for each missing relative. Those skulls were then used to represent lost loved ones, allowing families to perform ritual cremation and thereby possess

STATISTICS ON MASS GRAVE SURVEYS, 1995–1999

Province	Graves per District	Graves per Prison	Victims per Grave	Victims per District	Victims per Prison
Banteay Meanchey	71	142	72	5,098	10,196
Battambang	134	134	35	4,649	4,649
Kampong Cham	190	234	58	11,026	13,571
Kampong Chhnang	393	524	81	31,644	42,192
Kampong Speu	194	388	16	3,042	6,083
Kampong Thom	179	239	87	15,476	20,635
Kampot	345	394	20	6,953	7,946
Kandal	46	39	204	9,346	7,908
Koh Kong	0	0	---	2,478	17,349
Kratie	2	8	1,906	2,668	13,339
Mondulkiri	0	1	0	0	0
Phnom Penh	0	0	0	0	0
Preah Vihear	N/A	N/A	N/A	N/A	N/A
Prey Veng	151	227	50	7,451	11,176
Pursat	435	167	24	10,610	4,081
Ratanakiri	4	33	70	256	2,300
Siem Reap	51	80	109	5,562	8,653
Kron Preah Sihanouk	190	95	5	867	433
Stun Treng	12	15	66	800	1,000
Svay Rieng	28	18	31	851	567
Takeo	86	108	39	3,368	4,210
Averages	**132**	**150**	**169**	**6,429**	**9,278**

Source: Documentation Center of Cambodia, "Table 2: Descriptive Statistics on Mass Grave Surveys, 1995–1999." www.mekong.net/cambodia/toll.htm.

symbolic remains with which they can conduct Buddhist ceremonies for their dead.

Although Cambodia's thousands of mass graves are thus seen by the country's ruling elite as rich in political symbolism, and by the country's ordinary citizens as rich in religious symbolism, the mass graves also convey historical facts crucial for any process of legal accountability. Whether or not the Killing Fields will be found to constitute genocide or crimes against humanity in a court of law depends in significant measure on how that court understands the origin and nature of Cambodia's mass graves.

Khmer Rouge Chief Jailer Gets Life in Prison

Sopheng Cheang

After many years of controversy and legal wrangling, several of the highest-ranking surviving members of the Khmer Rouge faced trials before a United Nations tribunal in 2011 and 2012. In the following viewpoint, a journalist writes how the tribunal convicted one of them to life imprisonment in February 2012. The man convicted was Kaing Guek Eav, or "Duch." Duch was in charge of the torture and killing center in Phnom Penh known as Tuol Sleng, or Security Prison 21. Duch, who unlike fellow defendants Nuon Chea and Khieu Samphan admitted his crimes, was convicted of being responsible for at least 12,272 deaths as well as for torture and war crimes. Sopheng Cheang is a writer for the Associated Press.

Phnom Pehn, Cambodia (AP)—A U.N.-backed tribunal's Supreme Court lengthened the sentence for the Khmer Rouge's chief jailer to life imprisonment on Friday because of his "shocking and heinous" crimes against the Cambodian people.

The surprise ruling increased a lower court's 19-year sentence for Kaing Guek Eav, known as Duch. Prosecutors had appealed the sentence as too lenient, and outraged survivors had feared the man who oversaw the torture and killing of thousands could one day walk free.

Duch was the first defendant to be tried by the tribunal. He was commander of Phnom Penh's top-secret Tuol Sleng prison, code-named S-21. He admitted to overseeing the torture of his prisoners before sending them for execution at the "killing fields."

A coalition of 23 local civic groups, the Cambodian Human Rights Action Committee, welcomed Friday's decision and said Duch's victims had finally received justice.

In July 2010, the tribunal's lower court convicted Duch (pronounced DOIK) of war crimes, crimes against humanity, torture and murder.

He was sentenced to 35 years in prison but had 16 years shaved off for time served and other technicalities. The sentence was appealed both by prosecutors, who called for life imprisonment, and by Duch, who argued it was too harsh because he was merely following orders.

Judge Kong Srim, president of the Supreme Court Chamber, said Friday that the upper court felt the penalty should be more severe because the former jailer was responsible for the brutal deaths of so many.

"The crimes of Kaing Guek Eav were of a particularly shocking and heinous character based on the number of people who were proven to have been killed," the judge said. The tribunal says Duch oversaw the deaths of at least 12,272 victims but estimates have placed the number as high as 16,000.

The court said the high number of deaths and the extended period of time over which they occurred—from 1975 to 1979—"undoubtedly place this case among the gravest before international criminal tribunals."

Duch, 69, stood calmly without emotion as the sentence was read. He then pressed his palms together and drew them to his chest in a show of respect to the judge, before being led away by court guards. The ruling is final with no other chance for appeal.

Andrew Cayley, the British co-prosecutor, said Duch can request a pardon after serving 20 years, or about seven years from now.

Duch trained, ordered and supervised his staff to conduct "systematic torture and execution of prisoners" and showed "dedication to refining the operations of S-21, which was the factory of death," the court said in a separate statement.

Prosecutors called the ruling a long-awaited victory.

"We can say that justice has now been served after more than 30 years," Chea Leang said. "To us and to the victims, this is a great success."

The tribunal is seeking justice for an estimated 1.7 million people who died from torture, starvation, exhaustion or lack of medical care during the Khmer Rouge's rule in the 1970s.

Three senior Khmer Rouge figures are currently on trial in what is known as Case 002. Unlike Duch, who admitted his role and asked for forgiveness, the others claim no wrongdoing.

They are 85-year-old Nuon Chea, the Khmer Rouge's chief ideologist and No. 2 leader; 80-year-old Khieu Samphan, an ex-head of state; and 86-year-old Ieng Sary, the former foreign minister. They are accused of crimes against humanity, genocide, religious persecution, homicide and torture.

In its ruling Friday, the court said Duch did not deserve a lighter sentence just because he was not a senior Khmer Rouge official, and there was no rule that reserves the highest penalties for those at the "top of the chain of command."

That position reflects a key area of contention involving possible future trials. Cambodian Prime Minister Hun Sen has insisted the tribunal should end its operations after the current trial of the three senior leaders.

Human rights groups and international prosecutors, however, favor an extension of the proceedings to a third and fourth trial, where defendants would be second-level Khmer Rouge officials suspected of heinous crimes.

The matter has not yet been settled and has led to tension between the tribunal and the Cambodian government.

CHAPTER 2

Controversies Surrounding the Cambodian Genocide

Chapter Exercises

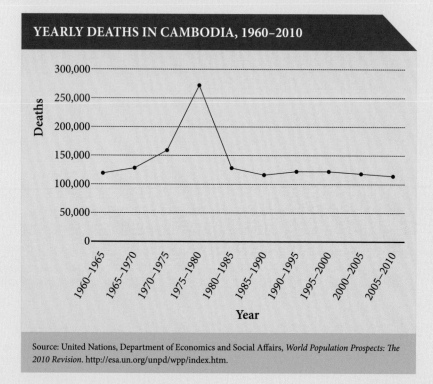

YEARLY DEATHS IN CAMBODIA, 1960–2010

Source: United Nations, Department of Economics and Social Affairs, *World Population Prospects: The 2010 Revision.* http://esa.un.org/unpd/wpp/index.htm.

1. Analyze the Graph

This line graph shows the annual death rate in Cambodia from 1960 to 2010 in hundreds of thousands and grouped into five-year periods.

Question 1: How much did yearly deaths increase in Cambodia from 1975 to 1980?

Question 2: Taking out the years of warfare and genocide from 1970 to 1980, what has been the normal range of the number of yearly deaths in Cambodia from 1960 to 2010?

Question 3: Because of the Cambodian genocide, the nation had a smaller total population in the 1980s than it did in the 1970s. How does this help explain why the yearly death rate was lower in the 1980s than it was in the 1960s or 1970s?

2. Writing Prompt

Write an editorial arguing that even though the United States may have helped create the conditions that brought the Khmer Rouge to power in Cambodia, the United States did not do so intentionally and cannot be blamed for Khmer Rouge atrocities.

3. Group Activity

Form two groups for the purpose of debate. One group should argue that it is best for Cambodia to continue to seek justice for the atrocities of the Khmer Rouge. The other group should argue that, after so many years, Cambodia should let go of the Khmer Rouge tragedy so it can move on.

Ex-Khmer Rouge Leader Blames U.S.

Seth Mydans

In the following viewpoint, a journalist reports in November 2011 on the claim by Khieu Samphan, one of the top Khmer Rouge officials, that the United States was largely responsible for bringing the Khmer Rouge to power. Samphan made the claim during a trial in which he was accused of war crimes and crimes against humanity in Cambodia. The basis for Samphan's claim comes from US participation in the Vietnam War, which spilled over the border into Cambodia in the early 1970s. The United States also helped bring about a military coup in Cambodia in 1970, which instituted leader Lon Nol. According to Samphan, support for Lon Nol as well as massive bombing raids that caused great upheaval in Cambodia's rural areas, inspired the rise of the Khmer Rouge. Seth Mydans covers Southeast Asia for the International Herald Tribune. *He has also worked for the* New York Times, Newsweek, *and the Associated Press.*

Phnom Penh—A Khmer Rouge leader told a court Wednesday that a secret campaign of U.S. bombing during the Vietnam War had contributed to the rise of the radical Communist movement that ravaged Cambodia three decades ago in one of the bloodiest episodes of mass killing in the last century.

The leader, Khieu Samphan, 80, the regime's head of state, also challenged the court to put former King Norodom Sihanouk on trial with him because the former king had previously held what Mr. Khieu Samphan called the same powerless titular position with the Khmer Rouge.

Mr. Khieu Samphan is one of three Khmer Rouge leaders charged in a U.N.-backed tribunal with genocide, war crimes and crimes against humanity that resulted in the deaths of 1.7 million people when they held power between 1975 and 1979.

"You seem to forget that between January 1970 and August 1973—that is, the period of two and a half years—the United States carpeted the small Kampuchean territory with bombs" in a campaign aimed at cutting off North Vietnamese infiltration into South Vietnam.

Kampuchea is the name used by the Khmer Rouge for Cambodia.

The bombing, together with a U.S.-backed coup that ousted then-Prince Sihanouk as head of state, inspired many Cambodians to join the Communist resistance, often responding to a call to arms by the prince.

"Could you imagine what my country faced after such a bloody killing and war?" asked Mr. Khieu Samphan. "Can you imagine what the situation was like for the Cambodian people and the country as a whole during such carpet bombings?"

A second defendant, Ieng Sary, 86, the former foreign minister, spoke only briefly on Wednesday, challenging the jurisdiction of the court and noting that he had received a royal pardon and amnesty when he surrendered from the Khmer Rouge guerrilla movement in 1996. The court has ruled that that amnesty does not apply to its proceedings.

"I'm very exhausted," said Mr. Ieng Sary, who has a variety of medical problems and was wheeled to the witness stand in a wheelchair.

The Vietnam War Spreads to Cambodia

Beginning in 1965, the United States engaged in a controversial military effort to stop the spread of communism to South Vietnam, and by 1968 there were more than a half million US troops there. The spread of this conflict to Cambodia is generally thought to have helped the Khmer Rouge become a major force in that country.

The border areas separating Vietnam and Cambodia were sparsely populated, and the border meant little to local populations, having only been established in 1954. North Vietnamese Communists, seeking to support their fighting in South Vietnam, often crossed the border on supply runs. Cambodian leader King Sihanouk not only permitted this, he gave the Vietnamese access to the port of Sihanoukville so that further supplies could enter.

After General Lon Nol's government ousted Sihanouk in 1970, both his Cambodian forces and the United States began a major effort to close off these supply routes as well as remove any encampments of Vietnamese Communists on the Cambodian side of

"I perhaps cannot continue reading because my heart will not allow me to continue reading," he said, putting a hand on his chest under his zippered jacket and sighing.

Like Mr. Khieu Samphan, the third defendant, Nuon Chea, 85, also sought to put the Khmer Rouge period into historical context when he spoke on Tuesday by saying it had been part of a struggle against Vietnamese ambitions to annex Cambodia and exterminate its people.

On Wednesday, one of Mr. Nuon Chea's lawyers, Michiel Pestman, issued a statement saying that Henry Kissinger, the former U.S. secretary of state, should also be put on trial for war crimes as "possibly the main architect of the bombing campaign in Cambodia."

the border. A force of some eighty thousand US and South Vietnamese troops invaded Cambodia on April 30, 1970. The attack was accompanied by large-scale US bombing raids.

The expansion of the Vietnam War to Cambodia had widespread effects. It resulted in major controversies in the United States, resulting in some of the largest antiwar protests of the Vietnam era. Many thought the invasion illegal, because there was no formal declaration of war. Indeed, President Richard Nixon had pledged to end the war in Vietnam, not expand it. Calls grew louder both among antiwar activists and in the US Congress for the conflicts in Southeast Asia to be brought to a rapid close.

In Cambodia, the effects of the Vietnam War were drastic. North Vietnamese troops occupied parts of Cambodia as far westward as Angkor Wat and reestablished their positions in border regions. In response, the United States expanded its bombing campaign. Meanwhile King Sihanouk's supporters entered into a temporary alliance with others who resented both the Lon Nol government and its US supporters. These included North Vietnam's powerful forces and the mysterious Khmer Rouge, which was finding increasing support among rural people uprooted by invasion and bombing.

"Most historians agree that without this American intervention the Khmer Rouge would not have been able to seize power," Mr. Pestman said. "Without Kissinger we would not be here today."

The references to U.S. culpability are clearly aimed at the public and the historical record, since the charges in this case are strictly limited to the Khmer Rouge period in power from 1975 to 1979.

In the tribunal's first case, Kaing Guek Eav, or Duch, the commandant of the main Khmer Rouge prison, Tuol Sleng, was sentenced in July 2010 to 35 years, commuted to 19 years.

Mr. Khieu Samphan, who before going underground was a teacher and legislator known for riding his bicycle to Parliament in a gesture of frugality, spoke forcefully about his ideals and his innocence, gripping his typed remarks with both hands and holding them up at eye level.

"I continue to hope that this trial will at least give me an opportunity to explain to the Cambodian public how it was possible for me to have occupied an official senior position in Democratic Kampuchea without having been a part of the decision-making process and without having been informed of all that was happening in our country," he said.

"Why is there no document confirming that I was an official member of the Standing Committee?" he asked, denying that he was part of the decision-making group in which membership would be evidence of guilt.

"You would have the public believe that everyone is lumped together in the same bag," he said. "But it's a lie. A manipulation. In fact you know very well that Democratic Kampuchea was very structured, compartmentalized and had a penchant for secrecy."

Rebutting the prosecutors' contention that he must have known about atrocities because he had often traveled through the country, Mr. Khieu Samphan said, "Do you really think that when I visited these work sites, alone or accompanied by the king, workers were being murdered in front of us with hoes or bullets in the back of the neck?"

He disparaged the prosecutors' claim that party leaders were responsible for an abusive policy of forced marriage, in which reluctant couples were sometimes spied on to confirm that they had consummated their union.

"Of course I wasn't a member of the 'angkar,'" he said, using the word applied to the shadowy Khmer Rouge leadership, and then, looking out from behind his sheaf of papers, "but I imagine that with a country to run, that its members had other things to do than to check if people were having sex."

He called the prosecutors "monumentally biased" and said he was in the courtroom to set the record straight. The defen-

US planes drop bombs near the Cambodian capital in 1973. Some believe the bombings by the United States during the Vietnam War helped the Khmer Rouge gain power. © AP Images.

dants will be given several opportunities to address the court again as it explores various aspects of the charges.

"I believe that the more procedures at the court evolve, the more the monks and the public will see and understand and judge the issues for themselves," he said.

As in previous sessions, the courtroom was packed with villagers who had been bused from the provinces and with groups of white-shirted students.

One of the students, Dany Sang, 22, a teacher trainee, said: "I don't know about the past, but I just listen. I don't have the confidence to make a decision. I will discuss it with my teachers or my parents because they know about the things in the past. Now, I'm not clear."

He said that he was convinced that the defendants wanted to help their country but that he did not believe Mr. Khieu Samphan's assertion that he was ignorant of the killings.

"The Khmer Rouge were not good," he said. "They killed a lot of people. A lot of people hate them so much. Me, too. They killed our relatives, our nation. I really hate them."

Khmer Rouge Leaders Must Take Responsibility for Their Own Crimes

Henry Kamm

In the following viewpoint, a journalist argues that the leaders of the Khmer Rouge must be considered responsible for the crimes committed during the Cambodian genocide. The author pieces together the motivations of Khmer Rouge leaders, tracing their history and participation in radical politics in France in the 1950s. But ultimately, he is unable to conclude that leaders, most notably "Brother Number One" Pol Pot, were interested in anything other than personal power as opposed to a political or social ideal. Henry Kamm is a reporter on Asian affairs and author of Dragon Ascending: Vietnam and the Vietnamese *and* Cambodia: Report from a Stricken Land.

The regime's lies were monstrous, of dimensions to match [Nazi Germany's propaganda chief Joseph] Goebbels's, but because of the total absence of public information they did not reach the Cambodian people, those who would have been best able to measure Pol Pot's spectacular perversions of the truth. "We lived like frogs at the bottom of a well," an agricultural engineer said after the liberation, describing the state of ignorance

Henry Kamm, "The Genocide and Its Perpetrators," *Cambodia: Report from a Stricken Land.* New York: Arcade Publishing, 1998, pp. 134–143. Copyright © 1998 by Henry Kamm. All rights reserved. Reproduced by permission.

in which Cambodians were kept, ignorance even of their leaders' infrequent public pronouncements.

Speaking to a group of rare foreign visitors, a "delegation" of Yugoslav journalists, in March 1978, the despot who ruled over a country where untold numbers of people were dying daily of hunger and malaria asserted brazenly that the problem of rice production had been solved and there was "enough rice to feed our people." And, Pol Pot continued, "We have eliminated malaria." He went on to boast of one more fictitious achievement: "Another outstanding result is the basic elimination of the illiteracy, which was a blemish in the former society." This from the head of the regime that had abolished the entire system of education. The unwritten conventions governing journalistic good manners between "brotherly" Communist nations, applied even by the less orthodox Yugoslavs, barred the unbelieving "delegates" from following up with skeptical questions. They did not raise the fundamental issue of whether there was truth in the harrowing descriptions of life in "Democratic Kampuchea," as the regime had renamed the country—they asserted "Cambodia" was a colonialist term—that the testimony of refugees had presented to the world. Privately my Yugoslav colleagues told me that they were horrified even by the prettified glimpses of reality that lurked behind what they were shown during their carefully staged, constantly supervised visit.

The Pol Pot Regime Had Unclear Ideas and Motivations

What motivated the Pol Pot regime to set in motion and continue in the face of appalling results its unique, murderous experiment in social engineering, will, I believe, remain forever an enigma. Not being intellectuals or theorists, Pol Pot, Ieng Sary, Nuon Chea, Son Sen, and the others have provided no writings that might explain their thought. The 1959 Sorbonne doctoral dissertation of Khieu Samphan, another Pol Pot disciple, on the outlook for industrialization in Cambodia is, to say the least, of little relevance to the economically destructive rustication of an entire nation that the Khmer Rouge government imposed. There was nothing resembling [Chinese Communist leader] Mao Zedong's collection of moralizing platitudes bound in red [Mao's "Little Red Book"], although the Cambodian leaders had probably read it and nodded approvingly at its revolutionary banalities.

Pol Pot's extremely rare public declarations in his four years in power were couched in the wooden language of ill-digested Marxism-Leninism. They were reminiscent of Stalin's paternalistic pronouncements and writings while millions of Soviet citizens were dying of starvation in the countryside or in the terrors of his gulag, either blatant lies or verbiage conveying no meaning. Whether Pol Pot's statements were intentionally obscurantist or an authentic reflection of an intellect dulled by decades of hearing and speaking only theoretical revolutionary claptrap remains a mystery.

I have had a half-dozen or so substantial conversations with Pol Pot's deputy in government, Ieng Sary, in various capitals, in jetliners, and in a jungle encampment, between 1973 and 1997. He is the only member of Pol Pot's inner circle who has spoken extensively to outsiders and given an image, however self-serving, of how the Khmer Rouge leadership functioned. Our conversations disclosed little to elucidate the political philosophy of the deputy prime minister in charge of foreign affairs, if there ever was one other than paranoiac hatred of Vietnam, where he was born. Immediately after the Vietnamese had driven Pol Pot's regime of Democratic Kampuchea from Phnom Penh, Ieng Sary made his first admission of some of the gravest charges that had been laid against it. He had rejected them indignantly in the past.

"In the early days there was certainly much killing," he told me a few hours after he had fled into Thailand as the Vietnamese columns neared the border region in January 1979. A Thai commercial flight was taking him from Bangkok to Hong Kong on his way for a visit to Beijing. A few months later, when again I had occasion to travel with him, on a flight from Bangkok to Sri

Lanka, he said dismissively that the number of those killed in the four Khmer Rouge years was only "a few thousand." When the hostess came pushing her wagon of duty-free goods into the first-class compartment, a touch of surrealism entered with her. The radical revolutionary, right out of a Khmer Rouge encampment in the deep forest, took considerable time in choosing among various perfumes, questioning the stewardess about their qualities. He made his purchase with some of the American currency that China was providing to keep Khmer Rouge militancy buoyant.

Thoughts of a Former Khmer Rouge Leader

Early in 1980, Ieng Sary was far more loquacious and seemed to draw closer to at least a partial truth during a two-hour conversation. I had accepted an invitation to spend two days at a secret jungle base in northern Cambodia, near the Thai border. We sat alone and talked by the light of a smoky kerosene lamp deep into the night, after a banquet offered by him and Khieu Samphan. "There were political errors," my host said in his lisping voice. "We recognize there were errors in going too far to the left. We moved too rapidly. We did not think enough about the organization of the state. We emphasized the political consciousness too much and had too little experience in the management of the state. We did not choose our public servants well and lost some control. Each region constituted a small kingdom. They ran their own affairs."

The deputy prime minister made a far from credible or creditable attempt to dissociate himself from the expulsion of the city populations. "Phnom Penh was liberated on April 17, and I arrived from China April 24," he said. "The city was already evacuated. It was a collective decision. If there had been two or three who think like me the decision would not have been taken." He added that Pol Pot had been "the leading personality" in the making of the decision. His implication that so fundamental a policy had been decided not well in advance by the party leadership but at the very last moment—the expulsion was decreed on the day that Phnom Penh was conquered—is impossible to credit. Ieng Sary was certainly part of the inner council that ruled on matters of such importance. (He was not, however, the second in command in the all-important Communist party of Cambodia. He held that rank only in the Khmer Rouge government. I asked him at a meeting in Phnom Penh in 1997 what his real place had been in the party hierarchy. He had defected the year before from the Khmers Rouges and been recognized by Hun Sen, Cambodia's latest strongman and a much earlier defector, as an independent warlord in a particularly rich border area. "Number Six," he replied modestly.)

Ieng Sary made it clear that the inner council around Pol Pot, whose title was party secretary, actively discussed important policies, and Pol Pot did not rule alone. He said that he had "raised many questions" about the abolition of money but had been told by Pol Pot that Cambodians did not know how to handle it. He grew agitated in his rather ignoble effort at white-washing himself by pushing the guilt for the most cruel policies on Pol Pot and others close to him, exempting himself. "I defended the intellectuals and was accused of being a rightist who knew nothing of the country because I had lived in exile," he said. He was referring not to his student days in Paris but his 1970–75 assignment in Beijing as the Khmer Rouge "ambassador" to Sihanouk, the wartime nominal chief of the anti-Lon Nol alliance. "There was no real discussion between Sihanouk and me," he told me. "He regarded me as a spy," a valid testimony to the prince's political acumen.

A Leadership Group Evolves

I met Ieng Sary again at the end of 1980. By then he was ready to concede that the regime's "errors" had been on a large scale. "We made a revolution," he said, in a hotel room in Jakarta. "The revolution in Vietnam and in France made many errors, too; many good things and many errors. We tried." When I asked him to

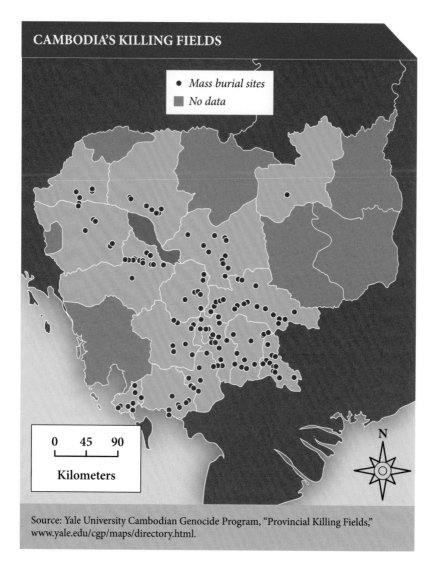

CAMBODIA'S KILLING FIELDS

- Mass burial sites
- No data

0   45   90
Kilometers
N

Source: Yale University Cambodian Genocide Program, "Provincial Killing Fields,"
www.yale.edu/cgp/maps/directory.html.

describe some of the "good things," he was at a loss and finally called on an associate to fill the awkward gap. "Agricultural progress," was the best Minister for Economy and Finance Thiounn Thioum could think of, a claim belied by the state of the country that I had toured earlier in the year.

By 1997 Ieng Sary had advanced sufficiently in his divorce from his ideological past to give further insights into relations within the leadership. He sought to separate himself more emphatically than earlier from Pol Pot. He said that his differences with the party leader, who was as we talked a prisoner of his comrades Nuon Chea and Ta Mok in a northern redoubt, had begun after both had returned from government scholarships that took them to Paris after 1945. There, from 1951 until 1956, Ieng Sary had been head of the cell of the French Communist party for Cambodian students. Pol Pot was "a simple member," Ieng Sary said. Pol Pot returned to Cambodia in 1953; his scholarship had been canceled after he failed to attend his courses in electrical engineering regularly. Ieng Sary returned home in 1957. "There was a very important political discussion between Pol Pot, Son Sen, and myself in 1960," he said. Son Sen, the Khmer Rouge defense minister, had also belonged to the group of Cambodian Communist students in France. The issue was "national democracy," which Ieng Sary said he advocated. "But Pol Pot was against democracy," he said.

They shared a common past in France, where the anticolonialism and republicanism of the young Cambodian nationalists found a facile theoretical basis in Communist ideology and an organizational home in the French party. A strong bond was forged, and apparently considerable freedom of speech prevailed among Pol Pot, Ieng Sary, Son Sen, Khieu Samphan, and a handful of others who became the leaders of their country. Some ended as victims at Tuol Sleng, the torture and assassination center in Phnom Penh. The group also included the Khieu sisters: Khieu Ponnary, Madame Pol Pot until he divorced her and married a younger woman when she began to suffer from depression, and Khieu Thirith, who remains Madame Ieng Sary. As an example of the candor that prevailed among them, Ieng Sary recalled that, annoyed at Khieu Samphan's slavish devotion to Pol Pot even while Samphan held the title of head of state from 1976 until 1979, Madame Ieng Sary said to him, "You should talk back to him. You act like the head of his office, not like the head of state."

The French Colonial Legacy

Living in the stimulating and highly politicized atmosphere of Paris of the 1950s must have been an overwhelming experience for young people at a most impressionable age from sleepy Phnom Penh. They had had a thoroughly French education through high school, which equipped men and women of their generation in former French colonies with an admiring view of France as the intellectual center of the world, even while they resented France's colonial dominance in their countries. They had learned far more about French geography, history, and literature than about their own countries and tended to see the world through assimilated French eyes and sensibilities.

I have always been struck by the readiness of Cambodians, far greater than that of their Vietnamese or Laotian neighbors, to adopt and make their own foreigners' ideas, particularly when delivered in French. Their French comrades in Paris, with the perennial readiness of the left-wing French "intellectuals" to construct radical theories and order the lives of others, must have played an important role in shaping the radicalism of Democratic Kampuchea. At the very least they must have heightened the readiness of Pol Pot and those around him to absorb Soviet, Vietnamese, and Chinese revolutionary prescriptions.

Back from France, most of the Cambodian Communists found teaching jobs in Phnom Penh and busily organized revolutionary cells among students and urban workers. They remained barely ahead of the persecution of Sihanouk's brutal secret police, supervised by Lon Nol. In 1963, Ieng Sary recalled, Pol Pot, by then acting head of the Khmer Workers party, said the time had come for the leaders to go into the "maquis." Indochinese Communists all use the French World War II term "maquis" when they talk about creating or joining a resistance movement in the jungle. Ieng Sary, as a member of the Central Committee, had urged staying in Phnom Penh, saying "we could still work underground there." But Pol Pot insisted, and Ieng Sary accepted "on condition that we stay inside Cambodia." He feared

Vietnamese control over the Cambodian Communists; Hanoi was the revolutionary center of Indochina. Pol Pot learned many revolutionary lessons from the Vietnamese on his visits in 1965 and 1970, Ieng Sary said, "above all his secretiveness."

Was the suffering of the Cambodian people under the Khmer Rouge regime a secret to Ieng Sary? When did he learn of it? "From my children, in 1976," he replied. "All four lived in communes around Phnom Penh and were often sent to the countryside to gather herbs for traditional medicines. They came to me and said, 'Papa, people are dying of hunger. They are eating gruel, not rice.' I confronted Pol Pot, not at a meeting but in tête-à-tête [face to face] and questioned him. He said I was against the regime. From then on, whenever I came back from a foreign trip, when the plane approached Phnom Penh, I asked myself, 'Will I go home or to 21-A?'" He was referring to the notorious Tuol Sleng by its party code name, which was S-21 or 21-A.

The German Comparison

His apologia for his political life reminded me of the self-justifications that I had often heard in Germany at the end of World War II. People who clearly knew better claimed time and again they didn't know about concentration camps. Yet when asked why Hitler and the Nazis met no opposition, the same people replied: "How could we oppose them? We were all afraid of being sent to a concentration camp."

How much did Ieng Sary know about Tuol Sleng? I asked. "I thought it was a reeducation center, and after reeducation people would be sent back," he replied. "But later I noticed they didn't come back. I knew people were accused there without justification." And Pol Pot? I asked. Ieng Sary shrugged. "I don't know if Pol Pot knew. Only two people knew for certain, because they must have been there: Nuon Chea, who was responsible in the party for security, and Son Sen, who was responsible for state security." Those who have studied the rich archives of interrogation transcripts left behind at Tuol Sleng have no doubt that Pol Pot was fully aware of what purposes it served. Did Pol Pot intend the wanton mass killings, the starvation, the inhuman mistreatment? I asked Ieng Sary. Was he aware, while living in Phnom Penh, which was empty of people except those who served the party and government, of what life was like for Cambodians? Ieng Sary suggested that the leader may not have known the full truth or cared to know it. "Pol Pot spoke only in theory," his Number Two in government, Number Six in the Communist party, replied. "He was a master of words. He spoke convincingly at meetings."

With all their self-justification, Ieng Sary's words contain some plausibility. Like his direct predecessor, Lon Nol, Pol Pot traveled little outside the capital and had scarce direct knowledge of how Cambodians lived under his rule. I doubt that his underlings ever reported to him facts that would have contradicted the brilliant results of his policies that he claimed as his achievements. Nothing that Pol Pot has said publicly, in or out of power, indicates that he was interested in the effects of his rule on the Cambodian people. What motivated Pol Pot and mattered most to him, according to Ieng Sary, was "the fear of losing his power."

I will never know whether Ieng Sary's account of his conversation with Pol Pot about starvation in the countryside, where all Cambodians were forced to live, is true. But Pol Pot would not have been the first dictator in history to reject an associate's unpleasant report and accuse him of opposition.

The Leaders of Khmer Rouge Committed Genocide

The collective culpability of the Khmer Rouge leadership in the genocide of their own people is beyond doubt. Since 1979 I have not met a Cambodian, including ministers of the Khmer Rouge regime, who did not mourn the death of members of his family between 1975 and 1979. Nor is there any doubt that the executions without trial of entire classes of men and women were acts of determined policy.

Pol Pot's leadership is responsible also for having stirred up the insane and lethal hatred of many of the "old people," those who had been "liberated" by the Khmers Rouges earlier in the 1970–75 war, toward the "people of 1975." These were Cambodians of Phnom Penh, Battambang, and other towns and villages, the great majority of the population, who remained under the Lon Nol government's rule until the Communists' final victory. The youngest of the oppressors were the generation of malevolent children—mindless, brutal servants of the Pol Pot regime, who starved and worked to death hundreds of thousands of their compatriots, made countless others die of unattended maladies, and turned the lives of vast numbers into nameless terror from which they will not recover.

But I suspect that innumerable deaths and an infinity of suffering resulted also from the tendency of Cambodian leaders to give no thought to the ultimate results of policies that they dictate and the dangerously fatuous words in which they are communicated to those responsible for carrying them out. In such circumstances, a central decision to make the "people of 1975" experience the hardships and deprivation that the "old people" suffered during the war against Lon Nol and the United States Air Force; to make them obedient servants of Angkar [the Khmer Rouge regime], like the "old people"; to teach them to live like "true Cambodians" rather than as pampered "running dogs of American imperialism," could easily be translated in its transmission to half-educated regional chiefs and by them to the brainless automatons of their creation into a license to brutalize and murder by all means at their disposal.

Khmer Rouge Were Not Bad People, Former Leader Tells Court

The Guardian

In the following viewpoint, a British newspaper reports on the December 2011 United Nations tribunal of Khmer Rouge leader Nuon Chea. Chea sought to defend himself by denying Khmer Rouge involvement in atrocities against Cambodians. Claiming instead that the Khmer Rouge wanted to help Cambodia, Chea blamed the mass killings on Vietnam, which invaded Cambodia and ousted the Khmer Rouge in 1979. Chea was "Brother Number Two" to Pol Pot's "Brother Number One" in the hierarchy of Khmer Rouge leadership. He remained a powerful official in the Khmer Rouge until the end of the organization in 1999 and was finally arrested for alleged war crimes in 2007.

A former leader of Cambodia's brutal Khmer Rouge regime has told a court he and his comrades were not "bad people", denying responsibility for the deaths of 1.7 million people during their 1970s rule and blaming Vietnam for any atrocities.

Nuon Chea's defiant statements came as a UN-backed tribunal began questioning him and two other Khmer Rouge leaders in court for the first time.

The long-awaited trial began late last month with opening statements, and this week the court is expected to focus on charges involving the forced movement of people and crimes against humanity. After the Khmer Rouge captured Phnom Penh on 17 April 1975, they began moving an estimated 1 million people, including hospital patients, from the capital into the countryside in an effort to create a communist agrarian Utopia.

After a court clerk read a background of the Khmer Rouge and the three defendants, Nuon Chea defended the notoriously brutal former movement, in which he was the number two leader behind the late Pol Pot.

"I don't want the next generation to misunderstand history. I don't want them to believe the Khmer Rouge are bad people, are criminal," Nuon Chea said. "Nothing is true about that."

The 85-year-old communist movement's one-time chief ideologist said no Cambodian was responsible for atrocities during the Khmer Rouge's 1975–1979 reign, reiterating a claim that neighbouring Vietnam instead was responsible for mass killings. Vietnam, whose border suffered bloody attacks by Khmer Rouge soldiers, sponsored a resistance movement and invaded, toppling the Khmer Rouge in 1979 and installing a client regime.

"These war crimes and crimes against humanity were not committed by the Cambodian people," Nuon Chea said. "It was the Vietnamese who killed Cambodians."

The trio of defendants is accused of crimes against humanity, genocide, religious persecution, homicide and torture stemming from the group's reign of terror. All have denied wrongdoing.

The other two are Khieu Samphan, an 80-year-old former head of state who also told the court in November he bore no responsibility for atrocities, and 86-year-old Ieng Sary, who has said he will not participate in the trial until a ruling is issued on a pardon he received in 1996. The tribunal previously ruled the pardon did not cover its indictment against him.

There is concern that the accused could die before justice is achieved.

Three top leaders of the Khmer Rouge were on trial at a war crimes tribunal in December 2011. © AP Images/Heng Sinith.

The Khmer Rouge's supreme leader, Pol Pot, died in 1998 in Cambodia's jungles, and a fourth defendant, 79-year-old Ieng Thirith, was ruled unfit to stand trial last week because she has Alzheimer's disease. She is Ieng Sary's wife and served as the regime's minister for social affairs.

The tribunal is seeking justice on behalf of the estimated quarter of Cambodia's population who died from executions, starvation, disease and overwork under the Khmer Rouge.

"This is the first time the accused persons will be asked questions in a public hearing about their role in the events that led to the takeover of Phnom Penh on 17 April 1975 and about the policies of the Khmer Rouge," the tribunal spokesman Lars Olsen said.

Olsen said the initial testimony would take several days. After the accused have been questioned, witnesses and civil parties will be also called to testify, he said.

So far the UN-backed tribunal, established in 2006, has tried just one case, convicting Kaing Guek Eav, the former head of the

Khmer Rouge's notorious S-21 prison, last year and sentencing him to 35 years in prison for war crimes, crimes against humanity and other offences. His sentence was reduced to 19 years due to time served and other technicalities.

That case was seen as much simpler than those before the court, in part because Kaing Guek Eav confessed to his crimes.

Chum Mey, 80, one of only two survivors of the S-21 prison, said he did not believe the three defendants would tell the truth about what happened in the 1970s.

"During last month's sessions we heard them say only that their regime was good and worked for the entire people," Chum Mey said.

The United States and Great Britain Supported Pol Pot and the Khmer Rouge

John Pilger

In the following viewpoint, an Australian journalist traces the connections of the United States and Great Britain to the Khmer Rouge regime in Cambodia. According to the author, these connections began when US bombing raids during the Vietnam War devastated Cambodia's countryside and inspired support for the Khmer Rouge. The connections continued during the Khmer Rouge regime and the genocide in Cambodia from 1975 to 1979. Then, after the Khmer Rouge was overthrown in 1979, the author claims that the United States and Great Britain provided military and financial support to the Khmer Rouge in Cambodia's subsequent civil war. The author maintains that the United States and Great Britain did not support the Khmer Rouge because they endorsed the regime's policies, but because they shared a common enemy: Vietnam. John Pilger is the author of Aftermath: The Struggle of Cambodia and Vietnam *and* Hidden Agendas. *He has also made documentary films such as* Year Zero: The Silent Death of Cambodia *and* Cambodia: Return to Year Zero.

John Pilger, "How Thatcher Gave Pol Pot a Hand," *New Statesman*, April 17, 2000. Copyright © 2000 by New Statesman. All rights reserved. Reproduced by permission.

On 17 April [2000], it is 25 years since Pol Pot's Khmer Rouge entered Phnom Penh. In the calendar of fanaticism, this was Year Zero; as many as two million people, a fifth of Cambodia's population, were to die as a consequence. To mark the anniversary, the evil of Pol Pot will be recalled, almost as a ritual act for voyeurs of the politically dark and inexplicable. For the managers of western power, no true lessons will be drawn, because no connections will be made to them and to their predecessors, who were Pol Pot's Faustian [after the character Faust, of German legend, who makes a deal with the devil] partners. Yet, without the complicity of the west, Year Zero might never have happened, nor the threat of its return maintained for so long.

The United States Bombs Cambodia

Declassified United States government documents leave little doubt that the secret and illegal bombing of then neutral Cambodia by President Richard Nixon and Henry Kissinger between 1969 and 1973 caused such widespread death and devastation that it was critical in Pol Pot's drive for power. "They are using damage caused by B52 strikes as the main theme of their propaganda," the CIA director of operations reported on 2 May 1973. "This approach has resulted in the successful recruitment of young men. Residents say the propaganda campaign has been effective with refugees in areas that have been subject to B52 strikes." In dropping the equivalent of five Hiroshimas on a peasant society, Nixon and Kissinger killed an estimated half a million people. Year Zero began, in effect, with them; the bombing was a catalyst for the rise of a small sectarian group, the Khmer Rouge, whose combination of Maoism and medievalism had no popular base.

After two and a half years in power, the Khmer Rouge was overthrown by the Vietnamese on Christmas Day, 1978. In the months and years that followed, the US and China and their allies, notably the [Margaret] Thatcher government [in the United Kingdom], backed Pol Pot in exile in Thailand. He was the enemy of their enemy: Vietnam, whose liberation of Cambodia could never be recognised because it had come from the wrong side of the cold war. For the Americans, now backing Beijing against Moscow, there was also a score to be settled for their humiliation on the rooftops of Saigon [the loss of the Vietnam War in April 1975].

To this end, the United Nations was abused by the powerful. Although the Khmer Rouge government ("Democratic Kampuchea") had ceased to exist in January 1979, its representatives were allowed to continue occupying Cambodia's seat at the UN; indeed, the US, China and Britain insisted on it. Meanwhile, a Security Council embargo on Cambodia compounded the suffering of a traumatised nation, while the Khmer Rouge in exile got almost everything it wanted. In 1981, President Jimmy Carter's national security adviser, Zbigniew Brzezinski, said: "I encouraged the Chinese to support Pol Pot." The US, he added, "winked publicly" as China sent arms to the Khmer Rouge.

In fact, the US had been secretly funding Pol Pot in exile since January 1980. The extent of this support—$85m from 1980 to 1986—was revealed in correspondence to a member of the Senate Foreign Relations Committee. On the Thai border with Cambodia, the CIA and other intelligence agencies set up the Kampuchea Emergency Group, which ensured that humanitarian aid went to Khmer Rouge enclaves in the refugee camps and across the border. Two American aid workers, Linda Mason and Roger Brown, later wrote: "The US government insisted that the Khmer Rouge be fed . . . the US preferred that the Khmer Rouge operation benefit from the credibility of an internationally known relief operation." Under American pressure, the World Food Programme handed over $12m in food to the Thai army to pass on to the Khmer Rouge; "20,000 to 40,000 Pol Pot guerillas benefited," wrote Richard Holbrooke, the then US assistant secretary of state.

I witnessed this. Travelling with a UN convoy of 40 trucks, I drove to a Khmer Rouge operations base at Phnom Chat. The base commander was the infamous Nam Phann, known to relief workers as "The Butcher" and Pol Pot's [Heinrich] Himmler [Nazi Germany's security chief]. After the supplies had been unloaded, literally at his feet, he said: "Thank you very much, and we wish for more."

Cambodia's Role in the Cold War

In November of that year, 1980, direct contact was made between the White House and the Khmer Rouge when Dr Ray Cline, a former deputy director of the CIA, made a secret visit to a Khmer Rouge operational headquarters. Cline was then a foreign policy adviser on President-elect Reagan's transitional team. By 1981, a number of governments had become decidedly uneasy about the charade of the UN's continuing recognition of the defunct Pol Pot regime. Something had to be done. The following year, the US and China invented the Coalition of the Democratic Government of Kampuchea, which was neither a coalition nor democratic, nor a government, nor in Kampuchea (Cambodia). It was what the CIA calls "a master illusion". Prince Norodom Sihanouk was appointed its head; otherwise little changed. The two "non-communist" members, the Sihanoukists, led by the Prince's son, Norodom Ranariddh, and the Khmer People's National Liberation Front, were dominated, diplomatically and militarily, by the Khmer Rouge. One of Pol Pot's closet cronies, Thaoun Prasith, ran the office at the UN in New York.

In Bangkok, the Americans provided the "coalition" with battle plans, uniforms, money and satellite intelligence; arms came direct from China and from the west, via Singapore. The non-communist fig leaf allowed Congress—spurred on by a cold-war zealot Stephen Solarz, a powerful committee chairman—to approve $24m in aid to the "resistance".

Britain's Connection with the Khmer Rouge

Until 1989, the British role in Cambodia remained secret. The first reports appeared in the *Sunday Telegraph*, written by Simon

"*Laos! Cambodia! Why can't
we stay in Vietnam, where we belong?*"

O'Dwyer-Russell, a diplomatic and defence correspondent with close professional and family contacts with the SAS [the elite force of the British military]. He revealed that the SAS was training the Pol Pot-led force. Soon afterwards, *Jane's Defence Weekly* reported that the British training for the "non-communist" members of the "coalition" had been going on "at secret bases in Thailand for more than four years". The instructors were from the SAS, "all serving military personnel, all veterans of the Falklands conflict [between the UK and Argentina in 1982], led by a captain".

The Cambodian training became an exclusively British operation after the "Irangate" arms-for-hostages scandal broke in Washington in 1986. "If Congress had found out that Americans were mixed up in clandestine training in Indo-China, let alone with Pol Pot," a Ministry of Defence source told O'Dwyer-Russell, "the balloon would have gone right up. It was one of those classic Thatcher-Reagan arrangements." Moreover, Margaret Thatcher had let slip, to the consternation of the Foreign Office, that "the more reasonable ones in the Khmer Rouge will have to play some part in a future government". In 1991, I interviewed a member of "R" (reserve) Squadron of the SAS, who had served on the border. "We trained the KR in a lot of technical stuff—a lot about mines," he said. "We used mines that came originally from Royal Ordnance in Britain, which we got by way of Egypt with marking changed. . . . We even gave them psychological training. At first, they wanted to go into the villages and just chop people up. We told them how to go easy. . . ."

The Foreign Office response was to lie. "Britain does not give military aid in any form to the Cambodian factions," stated a parliamentary reply. The then prime minister, Thatcher, wrote to [Labour Party leader] Neil Kinnock: "I confirm that there is no British government involvement of any kind in training, equipping or co-operating with Khmer Rouge forces or those allied to them." On 25 June 1991, after two years of denials, the government finally admitted that the SAS had been secretly training the "resistance" since 1983. A report by Asia Watch filled in the detail: the SAS had taught "the use of improvised explosive devices, booby traps and the manufacture and use of time-delay devices". The author of the report, Rae McGrath (who shared a joint Nobel Peace Prize for the international campaign on landmines), wrote in the *Guardian* that "the SAS training was a criminally irresponsible and cynical policy".

The Khmer Rouge's Connection with the United Nations

When a UN "peacekeeping force" finally arrived in Cambodia in 1992, the Faustian pact was never clearer. Declared merely a "warring faction", the Khmer Rouge was welcomed back to Phnom Penh by UN officials, if not the people. The western politician who claimed credit for the "peace process", Gareth Evans (then Australia's foreign minister), set the tone by calling for an "even-handed" approach to the Khmer Rouge and questioning whether calling it genocidal was "a specific stumbling block".

Khieu Samphan, Pol Pot's prime minister during the years of genocide, took the salute of UN troops with their commander, the Australian general John Sanderson, at his side. Eric Falt, the UN spokesman in Cambodia, told me: "The peace process was aimed at allowing [the Khmer Rouge] to gain respectability."

The consequence of the UN's involvement was the unofficial ceding of at least a quarter of Cambodia to the Khmer Rouge (according to UN military maps), the continuation of a low-level civil war and the election of a government impossibly divided between "two prime ministers": Hun Sen and Norodom Ranariddh.

The Hun Sen government has since won a second election outright. Authoritarian and at times brutal, yet by Cambodian standards extraordinarily stable, the government led by a former Khmer Rouge dissident, Hun Sen, who fled to Vietnam in the 1970s, has since done deals with leading figures of the Pol Pot era, notably the breakaway faction of Ieng Sary, while denying others immunity from prosecution.

Once the Phnom Penh government and the UN can agree on its form, an international war crimes tribunal seems likely to go ahead. The Americans want the Cambodians to play virtually no part; their understandable concern is that not only the Khmer Rouge will be indicted.

The Cambodian lawyer defending Ta Mok, the Khmer Rouge military leader captured last year, has said: "All the foreigners involved have to be called to court, and there will be no exceptions . . . Madeleine Albright, Margaret Thatcher, Henry Kissinger, Jimmy Carter, Ronald Reagan and George Bush . . . we are going to invite them to tell the world why they supported the Khmer Rouge."

Isolation Has Worsened the Suffering of Cambodians

Eva Mysliwiec

In the following viewpoint, a Cambodian activist describes how continued instability and international isolation prevented Cambodians from recovering fully from the genocide in the 1970s. Cambodia continued to suffer from a civil war in the 1980s that was fought among Vietnamese invaders, remnants of the Khmer Rouge, and other interest groups. Due to the continued presence of the Vietnamese, the author writes, international organizations and foreign governments avoided allowing outside aid to enter the country. In addition, Cambodia found it difficult to export to international markets or receive necessary imports. Burdens fell most notably on women, because so many men died in Cambodia's conflicts as well as the Khmer Rouge genocide. Eva Mysliwiec manages the advocacy organization Youth Star Cambodia.

The Kampuchean people continue to suffer not only from physical illness but from unhealed emotional scars left from so many years of oppression, abuse and the loss of family members and friends. An NGO [nongovernmental organization] representative states that in the five years she has spent in

Kampuchea, she has met only one person who claimed that he had not lost any family member during the tragic decade of war and the Khmer Rouge reign of terror. Foreign health personnel and aid workers find that emotional and psychological problems affect not only the general population but their Khmer counterparts at all levels of the administration. The Kampucheans no longer relate their tragic experiences to foreigners as compulsively as they did back in 1979 and 1980 but when memories are touched tears still come easily. There is no mistaking the terrible pain which is etched on the faces of many Kampucheans. The problems manifest themselves through depression and chronic grief, through the recurrence of nightmares, anxiety and fear of being exposed. Other symptoms of this debilitating illness include lack of motivation and difficulty in planning and organising work, as well as an inability to generate enthusiasm and hope for the future. A Khmer woman in Phnom Penh confessed to an NGO official, "I have a cloth hanging up in my home that says, 'to live is to hope'. I look at that every morning. Sometimes I want to tear it down and wrap it around my neck. But I know I must have hope for the sake of my children."

Lasting Insecurity in Cambodia

The recurring attacks launched by the opposition forces of which the Khmer Rouge are the strongest and most feared, only aggravate the insecurities of the Khmer people and fuel their all-pervading fear of the return of Pol Pot. Most Kampucheans find it incomprehensible that the UN supports the Coalition which the Khmer Rouge dominates, and that most nations of the world continue to give diplomatic recognition to their enemy, the Khmer Rouge. They do not understand why a majority of western governments appear to have turned their backs on the people of Kampuchea. The combination of fear and insecurity about the future, as well as the experiences under Pol Pot, also affect people's ability to take decisions, to criticise the system constructively when offered the opportunity to do so or to expose injustices. Under the Khmer Rouge such behaviour was often punishable by death. "The best policy" said the head of one technical department, "is just to keep a low profile and mind your own business. I have lived through four regimes. I lived under the king, I lived under Sihanouk, I lived under Lon Nol and the American bombing, I lived under Chinese-influenced Pol Pot, and now I live under the Vietnam-supported Heng Samrin. Who knows what tomorrow will bring and what I will be held accountable for?"

The fragile political climate also creates uncertainties. According to one Khmer, "Our country has no freedom. Our leaders speak well; their ideology is good, but they don't live up to their own ideas. And we cannot say anything."

The wounds of the past are not being allowed to heal and the Khmer people's efforts to build a future are undermined and frustrated by the ongoing conflict and ban on UN and western development aid. The conflict diverts men and financial resources away from reconstruction and agricultural production to defence work. As a result military conscription has recently been extended from three to five years and thousands of Khmer people from peasants to top administrators are deployed for 'patriotic works'. These include border defence and clearing brush in the forests and along the roads to deny access to Khmer Rouge guerillas and to protect military convoys from ambush.

Provision of all normal services is disrupted. For example, half the health personnel from Kampong Cham province were sent to perform their 2 month duty at the border, leaving the already understaffed hospital and health facilities even more handicapped. The war is also taking its toll on the already imbalanced adult population ratio, reducing the number of men even further and increasing the number of handicapped and amputees. A restaurant owner in Phnom Penh claims that anywhere from 200 to 300 amputees a day come in threatening to damage the premises if they are not given a few riels [the Cambodian currency]. Another Khmer, when asked what he saw as the future

Kampuchea answered with a prediction that circulated during the time of Pol Pot's regime: "The war will be over when every man has forty wives"—because most of the men will have been killed, he explained. The war also creates heavier burdens for peasants who must support those involved in defence work with 'patriotic contributions'—a part of their harvest.

The Kampuchean people also suffer from spiritual fatigue as a result of the ongoing conflict. They want serenity and time to enjoy their families and improve their lives. Many aid workers in Kampuchea have witnessed the emotional and physical strain under which their colleagues often work. For some, rest comes only when they have worked 7 days a week 18 hours a day for so long that they eventually suffer a breakdown and must be admitted to a hospital.

The Burden Falls on Cambodian Women

Women bear a disproportionate burden as a consequence of the Khmer Rouge regime and the continuing war. The demographic changes which by 1979 resulted in a higher proportion of women to men and a large number of widows, have added considerably to their difficulties. A survey in 1986 in Phnom Penh showed that from a random sample of 217 families, 53 were headed by women. Of these women heads of households, 91% were widows. Women are having to assume more responsibility in raising their families alone and having to undertake not only their own traditional tasks but those of the men as well.

Traditionally, men and women in Kampuchea assume different roles and functions. A majority of Kampucheans are involved in agriculture, but jobs that require more strength such as ploughing and harrowing or operating a *rohat,* a pedal-pushed irrigation wheel, are traditionally men's jobs. Similarly, house building and repairs were also considered men's work. Today women are found doing all of these jobs and during the planting season one sees many more women than men in the rice fields. This transition has not been easy for most women, who feared

Reconstructing Cambodia

The Khmer Rouge was ousted in early 1979 by a Vietnamese invasion, but Cambodia has yet to achieve full political stability even in the twenty-first century. From 1979 to 1989, a regime supported by Vietnam governed the country from Phnom Penh. But it was opposed by a coalition that included remnants of the Khmer Rouge, the supporters of former King Sihanouk, and other factions. The continued instability continued to create refugees and greatly discouraged foreign aid or investment.

Vietnamese troops withdrew in 1989 and with the help of the United Nations the opposing factions reached an agreement in 1991. This agreement provided for a United Nations Transitional Authority in Cambodia (UNTAC) that helped keep the peace, disarm opposing groups, assist refugees, and prepare the country for elections. These elections resulted in the formation of a new coalition government under Prime Minister Hun Sen. In 1993, Sihanouk was restored as king, although he had no real political authority.

In the late 1990s, following an attempted coup d'état, Hun Sen's government launched a violent oppression of remaining Communist factions, including the Khmer Rouge. Former Khmer Rouge leader Pol Pot, increasingly marginalized, died in a jungle hideout near the Thai border in 1998, while the last Khmer Rouge leaders abandoned their cause in 1999.

As of 2012, Hun Sen continues to govern, leading the Cambodian People's Party. He works closely with remaining members of the Cambodian monarchy. After King Sihanouk stepped down in 2004, his eldest son Norodom Sihamoni became king. Hun Sen's government has continued to drag its heels on one of the key issues connected with the Cambodian genocide: the trials of surviving leaders of the Khmer Rouge.

Cambodia's economic recovery has been slow, partly because the Khmer Rouge massacred so many of the country's educated people and devastated its agriculture; it remains among the world's poorest nations. Cambodia has come to rely on tourism stemming from the presence of Angkor Wat, one of the world's great ancient monuments. A sign of further possible recovery was the opening of the country's first stock exchange in April 2012.

that taking up traditionally male functions would make them less 'feminine' and reduce their chances of remarrying in a society with few men. The undereducation of women is a further disadvantage. In rural Kampuchea most women had less than six years of primary education, although before Pol Pot the number of women in higher education had been increasing.

Before the Khmer Rouge regime, most households depended on the combined efforts of both sexes and on the support of the extended family. But with the demographic imbalance many women found themselves the head of the household with no man to help with the domestic or financial burden. One woman agonized over how difficult it is now for women in Kampuchea, particularly those who have lost their husbands and parents. Women must live alone and must be totally responsible for their children. There is an unspoken understanding that because so many men have died, men can take more than one wife, and many have. In the words of this Khmer woman, "Relationships have changed very much; families used to be intact and supportive. Husbands and wives were loyal to each other. The men now are not good. They are deceitful and corrupt. They say one thing and do another. We can no longer trust each other."

Many women who come to the hospital for medical consultation suffer from depression, according to medical staff in Prey Veng's provincial hospital. They attribute this to the trauma of the Khmer Rouge period, the heavy responsibilities weighing on women, loneliness and the lack of marriage prospects for the future. During her research on women in Kampuchea in 1981, Chantou Boua, herself a Kampuchean woman living in Australia, found that:

> In Kampuchea today one often hears widows talking obsessively about their husbands, who were killed by Pol Pot forces. They talk about memories of earlier, happier days, about the dreadful Pol Pot period, about the abduction and killing of their husbands. It seems that, tragically, many women will

never forget the moment when their husbands were taken away or were shot or clubbed to death. These traumatic experiences haunt them and some women will never recover. . . .

Many women complain of how inefficient they are compared to earlier days. Bosses complain about their absent-minded and day-dreaming female employees. A peasant widow said, "I do not know what I am doing or thinking everyday, sometimes I forget about the pot of rice on the stove and leave it there to burn."

Today, except for the 'solidarity groups' which offer support to their most vulnerable members, there is almost nothing to help women cope with the emotional and psychological scars. "I just feel a deep sadness and very much alone", said one Phnom Penh women who lost her husband during the Khmer Rouge period. "When I get up in the morning I feel very heavy, like something is pressing on my shoulders. But I cannot talk to anyone. I have no friends. Oh yes, I have friends, but no one to whom I can say what I really feel."

An aid worker who participated in the Phnom Penh sanitation survey in 1986 found during house visits that some widows, or women who had no living relatives, lived together for mutual support and because they could not manage on their own.

The National Women's Association, which in the early 1980s had a highly political profile, has since 1984 modified its role and become more involved in addressing the problems of women, especially widows and women with limited education and skills. The Women's Association has been active in literacy programmes for women, in providing a number of skills training programmes for them, in organising sewing and weaving cooperatives, and helping them with income-generating projects such as the digging of fish ponds. They also provide some material assistance and support to women with children, whose husbands are fighting the war.

In view of the heavy burden and problems of women in Kampuchea today, it is disappointing to see the low priority given to programmes specifically geared to women's needs by Kampuchean government institutions and by the international agencies. However, UNICEF has increased its focus on women's programmes and their experience may lead to improvements in this area.

The Effects of Cambodia's Isolation

Closely related to the psychological stresses experienced by the Kampuchean people is the sense of isolation they feel. Between 1975 and 1978 it was the Khmer Rouge who initiated a self-imposed isolation. Today, the Association of South East Asian Nations, China and the majority of western governments isolate Kampuchea because of the presence of Vietnamese troops in the country. Most governments ostracize the Vietnamese-backed government in Phnom Penh and since it is not recognized in the United Nations there are no diplomatic, and very few cultural or educational exchanges between Kampuchea and any non-communist nation, with the exception of India. The people's access to outside ideas and influence is further limited by the government's own restrictive policies. Consequently, Kampucheans live in a kind of vacuum, not knowing what is going on in the outside world or sometimes even within their own country.

Inside the country, though communications have improved over the last few years, they are still difficult. People came out of the Khmer Rouge period, having been deprived of news, education and books, with an insatiable hunger for knowledge and reading material. Yet there are few reading materials available. There are no foreign newspapers on sale in Kampuchea. Those the aid agency staff receive are highly coveted.

The country's isolation is a great disadvantage in trading on the international market. The delay in receiving economic data or journals means that they cannot compete with international prices when trading their goods because information is often months out of date. Unbiased news of international affairs is hard to come by but there is a widely read Khmer weekly newspaper which publishes not only information about current activities in Kampuchea and the region but also popular criticisms of the regime.

Perhaps the most cruel aspect of this isolation is that it prevents family reunification and makes communication with relatives abroad extremely difficult. Khmers who lost all documentation and personal mementoes during the Pol Pot era have no way of finding the addresses of relatives overseas. Khmers living abroad have no current addresses for their relatives in Kampuchea and often still do not even know whether they are dead or alive. The postal system in Kampuchea is still erratic and unreliable. Many Kampucheans, mindful of the punishment received by those who had associations with the West under the last regime, are today still afraid to admit that they have relatives abroad and in some cases have changed their names, which makes them even more difficult to track down with any mail. Even though some organisations have officially attempted to negotiate reunification programmes with the Kampuchean government, the current climate of international hostility towards Kampuchea drives such efforts to a dead end.

Although to some extent international isolation has strengthened the Kampuchean people and led them to rely more on their own capabilities and resources, it sets a number of obstacles in the path of food self-sufficiency and reconstruction. Because of its isolation, Kampuchea has missed out on the last two decades of developmental experience and research in agriculture, health, appropriate technology and many other fields. Khmers are denied desperately needed training and educational opportunities abroad, although in some cases their own government restrictions prevent them going. Japan, France, the US, the Netherlands and Israel, for example, all had extensive technical agriculture and rice research programmes in Kampuchea before the war. Much of the documentation from that work is presently not available in Kampuchea. Blueprints for buildings, sewers and water systems which were built by foreign companies and which

Extreme poverty in Cambodia continues into the twenty-first century. Some Cambodians earn their living as garbage pickers in a dump near Phnom Penh. © Alessandro Vannucci/Demotix/Demotix/Corbis.

have suffered much damage from the war and lack of maintenance are also hard to come by, as are topographical maps and soil studies needed for irrigation systems or for well-drilling.

Unofficial Help from Overseas

Once an integral part of the International Mekong Committee's Development Plan, Kampuchean participation and development assistance has been suspended since 1975. It is also barred from participating in many other international organisations and conferences. However more opportunities have been opening up recently through the aid of NGOs and UNICEF, such as sponsoring women to international women's conferences, or sending Khmer representatives to a sanitation seminar in India. Over the last two years more Kampucheans have been involved in educational trips abroad especially to India and more recently to the Philippines' International Rice Research Institute (IRRI) which could offer Kampuchea much help in restoring the many seed varieties lost during the Khmer Rouge regime and provide valuable and appropriate training.

Educational exchanges are invaluable to Khmer technical and professional staff who have been cut off from outside ideas in their fields of expertise since the early 1970s. Western aid workers in Kampuchea have found that Khmers return from such trips refreshed and enthusiastic and full of new ideas. One Khmer who returned from a visit to health facilities in India remarked how much more poverty there was in India than in Kampuchea and was very impressed with the self-help preventive health programmes that Indians were managing without external assistance.

Isolation and the embargo on development aid to Kampuchea also prevents the country from obtaining spare parts or repair manuals for equipment provided or purchased before the war from US, Chinese, Korean and other international companies. For example, many badly needed Massey Ferguson tractors stand idle in Battambang province, and Korean pumps in one of Prey Veng's pumping stations were restored by a group of NGOs at a phenomenal expense because replacement parts were unobtainable and had to be made to order.

NGO personnel working in Kampuchea feel that even the limited exposure they have with Kampucheans helps to decrease the Khmers' sense of isolation and abandonment, and increases their sense of security and international interest in their welfare. For many Kampucheans the presence of the small number of westerners working in Kampuchea on behalf of aid agencies represents a window to the outside and a glimmer of hope for their country. Several Khmers have told aid workers: "When you [humanitarian organisations] have to leave, it will be a warning that something bad is going to happen to us".

Many of the Khmer officials interviewed felt that the most damaging effect of western-imposed isolation is that it limits the options available to them in determining their future and pushes them to become more dependent on Vietnam and the Soviet

Union. "How can we practise self-determination if you [Western governments] do not give us any choices?" asked one official. Many western aid workers and visitors to Kampuchea have sensed a real eagerness from Khmers for international relationships and recognition. Many of Kampuchea's educated and technical people were trained abroad in France, China, the US, India, the UK and elsewhere, or were trained by the French in Phnom Penh. Today, they as well as younger people recently trained in the Eastern Bloc, reach out for friendship and assistance from the international agency staff. As Kampuchea's Prime Minister Hun Sen put it, "There are two sides to isolation". It hurts not only Kampuchea but the West as well.

Until there is a commitment to work for a negotiated settlement of the Kampuchean conflict, political games will continue to strangle the hopes of the Khmer people for a country that is once again at peace, independent and neutral.

30 Years Later, Fall of Phnom Penh Recalled

Boston.com

The following viewpoint details the problems faced by former Khmer Rouge fighters thirty years after their movement took over Cambodia. Many of these fighters were extremely young, as the Khmer Rouge actively recruited young people who had been uprooted in the countryside by US bombings or political unrest. While fighters were happy with the success of the Khmer Rouge at first, the viewpoint indicates that this happiness turned quickly to disillusionment as the brutality and violence of the regime became clear. In the years since, Khmer Rouge veterans continue to face poverty and alienation in their society.

Chamkar Ta Nget, Cambodia—Nai Oeurn had reason to celebrate. Cambodia's civil war was over, and as the 14-year-old Khmer Rouge guerrilla marched into the capital, Phnom Penh, he truly believed his country's rural poor had triumphed.

Thirty years later, after the "killing fields" and the death of one-sixth of the Cambodian population, his dream has come to this: collecting cow dung for a living, earning 90 cents for a 3-foot-high pile that takes five days to collect.

For him, as for many other Cambodians, the 30th anniversary of the fall of Phnom Penh on April 17, 1975, is an occasion to remember the thrill of victory while ruing its horrifying aftermath.

"The ideology we were taught was to clean up the rich and the corrupt, who used to drive cars and look down on peasants, and to send them to work in the rice fields," Nai Oeurn said.

It became a failed effort to demolish and rebuild the nation from scratch, and resulted in an estimated 1.7 million deaths by execution, starvation, overwork, or lack of medical care.

The Khmer Rouge leaders under Pol Pot declared 1975 to be "Year Zero" and set out to smash private ownership, money, the family structure, privacy—anything that smacked to them of the old Cambodia. But their ruthless efficiency couldn't fashion a functioning replacement, and in the end, all Cambodians were losers.

Among the biggest losers are guerrillas like Nai Oeurn, many of whom have moved back to their impoverished villages and face suspicious neighbors who still remember the Khmer Rouge days.

Khorn Prak says he was wounded 27 times in battle. When the Khmer Rouge were ousted by a Vietnamese invasion in 1979, he returned home to learn that his mother had died of illness in the years he had been away. Now, at 53, he farms and mends bicycles in a village north of Phnom Penh.

The struggle, he said, "brought me nothing but my wounds. It was bloody and useless."

Cambodia had already been dragged into the Vietnam War and heavily bombed by US warplanes by the time the Khmer Rouge rolled into Phnom Penh.

They had been besieging the capital for months. The city was teeming with refugees and lacked food and medicine. But to guerrillas from the countryside such as 20-year-old Chhaing Tek Ngorn, it looked unimaginably wealthy.

Now 50 and a farmer, he remembers nervously smiling civilians shouting "Long live the liberation army!"

Guerillas ride elephants used in war in 1981. Former Khmer Rouge veterans continue to be alienated in Cambodia. © Alex Bowie/Hulton Archive/Getty Images.

Almost immediately, however, the new occupiers began driving the populace into the countryside. Government military officers and high-ranking civil servants were executed. Khorn Prak said it took just a week to turn Phnom Penh into "a ghost town."

Like Nai Oeurn, he was a believer who took part in the expulsion because he had a deep faith in the Khmer Rouge's pledge to eliminate distinctions between rich and poor.

"I had no feeling, did not pity anything. I had no desire to possess anything," he said.

Pol Pot died in the jungle in 1998, and about a dozen top Khmer Rouge aides may face a UN-assisted tribunal later this year. The foot soldiers, however, have been left to make their own peace with the past.

Although they have generally been able to rejoin society, an "emotional barrier" still remains between them and other Cambodians from their era, said Youk Chhang, director of a center researching Khmer Rouge atrocities.

"Former Khmer Rouge and the victims are not socially integrated as yet, because the Khmer Rouge still remain a living symbol of evil in our society," he said.

Various Problems Have Delayed the Trials of Khmer Rouge Leaders

Chris Tenove

Bringing leaders of the Khmer Rouge to justice for the Cambodian genocide has proven difficult, a Canadian scholar argues in the following viewpoint. Cambodia's political instability in the 1980s and 1990s meant that Khmer Rouge leaders remained free people, and new leaders—some of which are former members of the Khmer Rouge—have hesitated on trying accused criminals according to international standards. Although political interference continues to make the staging of trials difficult, the author maintains that many Cambodians hope the trials will help them cope with the aftermath of their country's genocide. Chris Tenove is a doctoral candidate in political science at the University of British Columbia.

Nuon Chea lives in an unpainted wooden shack on stilts, near a sluggish creek that marks the boundary between Cambodia and Thailand. A plank staircase leads up into his home. Out front, next to the narrow dirt road, several men lounge in the shade. They claim to be farmers, but AK-47s rest at their feet. Inside, Nuon Chea sits in a sturdy wooden chair, dressed in a billowing white shirt, with his hands resting calmly in his lap and a metal cane leaning against his knee. He is in his early eighties with receding white hair, and his cheeks are slightly hollowed with age. He appears to be daydreaming—but when he turns to greet a visitor, his gaze is sharp and probing. He reaches for a bamboo fan, waves it briskly, and asks, "What exactly is it that you want to know?"

He has good reason to be guarded. Nuon Chea was second-in-command of the Khmer Rouge, responsible for one of the bloodiest regimes in history. The Khmer Rouge were driven by a toxic mixture of nationalism, Maoism and paranoia, and intent on creating a "pure" agrarian society. Between 1975 and 1979, they outlawed money, separated families, pillaged temples, killed those who were well-educated, and elevated simple villagers to positions of authority. The result was a ruined economy and widespread hunger, which in turn caused outbreaks of dysentery and tuberculosis. Rather than change their policies, Khmer Rouge leaders performed increasingly brutal purges of their imagined "enemies." To dispose of these unwanted elements, the regime created hundreds of prisons, torture centres and execution sites—the infamous "killing fields." An estimated 1.7 million people were executed or died of torture, starvation or disease.

After the Khmer Rouge were driven from power, they spent the next two decades waging an insurgency from Cambodia's hinterlands. Finally, in the late 1990s, they disbanded. Since then, former Khmer Rouge leaders like Nuon Chea have lived as free men.

That may soon change. In Phnom Penh, a bone-rattling 12-hour drive from Nuon Chea's home, an empty theatre is being converted into a courtroom where former Khmer Rouge leaders will be put on trial. A team of war crimes investigators, led by a Canadian prosecutor, is at work building the cases. No suspects have been announced, but Nuon Chea will almost certainly be one of them. As "Brother Number Two" of the Khmer Rouge—Pol Pot was known as "Brother Number One"—he is believed to have helped develop and oversee their deadly policies.

Documents have linked him to incidents of torture and execution. One former Khmer Rouge officer has accused him of having a prisoner's body exhumed and photographed, so he would have proof of the man's death.

Liver spots speckle Nuon Chea's high forehead and his chin shakes slightly when he speaks, but his voice is firm with authority. "If they invite, I will go and testify," he says. A smile tugs at the corners of his thin lips, as if he were amused by the possibility. "I will go and I will explain the real truth."

The man who will likely face Nuon Chea in that courtroom is a former Crown [Canadian government] attorney from Montreal. Since last July, Robert Petit has been sifting through decades-old documents and tracking down witnesses. If Nuon Chea is put on trial, it is up to Petit, his co-prosecutor Chea Leang, and their team of 15 lawyers and investigators to make sure that the charges stick.

For that to happen, Petit must race against time. It has been almost a decade since Pol Pot died. Ta Mok, a former commander known as "the Butcher," died last year. Other Khmer Rouge leaders, including Nuon Chea, are reportedly in poor health. So, too, are some of the witnesses needed to provide evidence against them. All of this may be why, on this Friday afternoon in late February, there is a battered and fatigued look in Petit's dark eyes. He distractedly spins a business card in his fingers and scratches at his salt-and-pepper goatee. "I apologize if I seem rude," he says, speaking with a faint French-Canadian accent, "but it's been a long week."

Contending with Misinformation and Corruption

Above Petit's computer hang pictures of two young children and a beautiful Rwandan woman, his wife. Petit says his wedding was the most important thing to happen to him in Rwanda, though it is also where he found his calling. He arrived in the central African country in 1995 as a seasoned criminal prosecutor—he had been a Crown attorney for eight years—but with little in-

© 2007 by Patrick Chappate and Cagle Cartoons.com.

ternational experience. When offered a position at the Rwandan war crimes tribunal, the first thing he did was crack open his atlas to see where he was going. "I couldn't find Rwanda anywhere," he chuckles. "The country is so tiny that it had disappeared into the crease between two pages." He walked the trails between huts in Rwandan villages, searching for witnesses and suspects for war crimes trials, and later went on to prosecute war crimes in Sierra Leone, East Timor and Kosovo.

What makes Cambodia different from these other post-war countries, he says, is that so few Cambodians understand why the starvation, disease and murder happened. "In Rwanda, if you were a Tutsi, you knew that you were being attacked by the Hutus because of your ethnic identity," Petit says. "But here, I am constantly asked, 'Why would Cambodians kill so many Cambodians?'"

That question plagues survivors of the Khmer Rouge era, but also younger generations. For three decades, history has been alternately distorted and avoided in public debate. Confusion about the past has been heightened by the fact that former Khmer Rouge leaders continue to proclaim their innocence. "People have a very deep need to try to understand what happened here," says Petit. "These trials will probably be the best chance to establish some historical record."

It's easy, then, to imagine the pressure the 45-year-old lawyer is under. Not only are these historic and complex cases, but the tribunal itself—the Extraordinary Chambers in the Courts of Cambodia (ECCC)—is an awkward compromise between international legal standards and Cambodian sovereignty. Cambodia has no tradition of judicial independence, and Prime Minister Hun Sen has not been willing to surrender control over his nation's most important trials. The ECCC was created with 10 years of fraught negotiation between the United Nations and the Cambodian government. From day one there have been rumours of political interference.

The latest accusation, from the Open Society Justice Initiative, a New York-based watchdog organization, is that Cambodian staff at the ECCC paid kickbacks to government officials in exchange for their positions. Cambodian judges denied the allegations, but the United Nations Development Programme is investigating. (Canada has pledged to give $2 million to the ECCC.)

What's more, the tribunal's work has been delayed because the ECCC's international and Cambodian judges have disagreed on the procedures that will govern the trials. Behind closed doors, judges have reportedly clashed over issues such as when the court can publicly disclose the identity of accused persons. In mid-March, the judges announced that they had reached agreement. Then a new obstacle arose. Cambodia's Bar Association revealed its plan to charge foreign defence lawyers nearly $5,000 to work at the ECCC for a year. The international judges say this fee will limit defendants' ability to choose their counsel, and they have refused to let the trials proceed until it is changed.

Petit says that he will walk away from the ECCC if its procedures don't meet internationally accepted legal standards. But he hopes the issues are resolved soon. Trials, which could begin in early 2008, would send an important message, says Petit. "Sooner or later, you will be held accountable for your crimes."

Hoping for Justice

This justice can't come early enough for Theary Seng. In 2005 she published a book on her ordeal called *Daughter of the Killing Fields*. She steels herself before describing being thrown in jail at age 7, along with her widowed mother and four older brothers. Because Seng's wrists and ankles were too small for the iron shackles that restrained other prisoners, it became her job to empty toilet buckets and search for extra food. Four months later, a Khmer Rouge cadre [official] executed her mother, then released Seng and her brothers. She went as a refugee to the United States.

Seng, 36, now directs the Center for Social Development in Phnom Penh, a local human rights organization. She believes that trials of former leaders like Nuon Chea could help Cambodian society address the painful legacies of the Khmer Rouge era. "We remain very much a broken people," says Seng, glancing at a shelf of reports detailing social problems from mental illness to domestic violence. "Many survivors have been unable to talk about their trauma, they keep it inside them like a hard seed."

By finally bringing the former leaders to justice, she says, the ECCC could help undermine Cambodia's "culture of impunity"—a general belief that people with power can flout the rule of law. However, she, too, fears interference from the government. Some members of the ruling Cambodian People's Party were once Khmer Rouge soldiers themselves, including Prime Minister Hun Sen. None of today's leading politicians were senior enough to warrant prosecution by Petit, Seng says,

Khmer Rouge survivors and family members take part in an emotional prayer ceremony at the Tuol Sleng Genocide Museum near the end the 2010 trial of Kaing Guek Eav. © Paula Bronstein/Getty Images News/Getty Images.

but embarrassing information could surface in the trials. And it's not just Cambodians who are nervous. China provided the Khmer Rouge with material support and training, and Chinese diplomats have reportedly put pressure on the Cambodian government to reign in the tribunal.

Still, Seng believes the tribunal can achieve some good. "Cambodians need a chance to reflect on what happened 30 years ago, and talk about how it is affecting us today."

Many Cambodians want more than talk. Pok Savoeuth, a 50-year-old farmer from Battambang province, stares intently at the picture of a young man with his hands lashed behind his back and one eye clotted shut. It is just one of hundreds of photographs of inmates who were tortured and then executed in Tuol Sleng, a torture centre that has been turned into a museum. "If we don't sentence the Khmer Rouge leaders, our anger will be coming to us over and over again," she says, trembling with emotion. "They must face the law."

Coming to Terms with the Past

Even some former Khmer Rouge soldiers agree. Ngem En joined the Khmer Rouge as a teenager and soon became a photographer at Tuol Sleng. He took pictures of prisoners after they were tortured or before execution, and his diligence later earned him a job as the personal photographer to the Khmer Rouge leaders. "I want to build a museum for reconciliation between Khmer Rouge and other Cambodians," he says, flipping through snapshots of Pol Pot, Nuon Chea and other leaders in uniform and at play. Like many former Khmer Rouge soldiers, Ngem En supports the tribunal because it lays responsibility for atrocities at the feet of the top leaders. Some experts worry that this approach reinforces a tendency in Cambodian society toward blind obedience and rigid hierarchy, a tendency that the Khmer Rouge exploited.

Ngem En's photos suggest he was on good terms with the Khmer Rouge leaders, but he insists that he had no choice but to follow orders. "During that time you could not protest or interfere with other people's work, or you would be killed," he says. "The leaders were responsible for great injustices, and the world needs to be shown their mistakes." About Nuon Chea, he adds, "He may try and do good now, but you can't change history."

While renovations take place in the Phnom Penh theatre-turned-courtroom, while Robert Petit gathers his documents and witness testimonies, Nuon Chea waits out his days in his bucolic retreat near the Thai border. How does he explain the deaths that occurred during his government's rule? He smoothes his loose white shirt and then says, "The problems began in 1862, when the French colonizers took control of Cambodia." He blames the French, he blames the Americans, and he blames an unnamed "foreign power"—presumably Vietnam. But he does not admit to any serious mistakes made by his own government. The number of deaths caused by the Khmer Rouge has been greatly exaggerated, he suggests. There may have been a few missteps, he admitted in a 2004 interview with the *Cambodian Daily*, "but in principle we were right."

When questions persist, Nuon Chea becomes irritated by the topic. He's old. He complains of high blood pressure. "I am a sick man," he says, and he grimaces as he shifts one of his swollen ankles. "I need to go lie down." Putting Nuon Chea on trial could help illuminate a dark chapter in Cambodia's history. But if Robert Petit and the people of Cambodia are going to get any answers out of this man, they'll have to act quickly.

Decisive Trials of Khmer Rouge Leaders May Mean That Cambodia Is Finally Coming to Terms with Its Genocide

James Pringle

In 2006, a United Nations–backed tribunal authorized trials of surviving Khmer Rouge leaders. Political squabbles and other delays put off conclusive trials, however, until 2011 and 2012. In the following viewpoint, a British journalist examines these trials and the possibility that they might allow Cambodia to come to terms with its genocide and move forward. The author focuses on the career, trial, and ultimate sentencing to life imprisonment of Kaing Guek Eav, or "Duch," who commanded the torture and killing center of Tuol Sleng in Phnom Penh. The author writes that a strong possibility still exists of political interference with the tribunal, but he indicates that the life sentence handed out to Duch has been the source of much satisfaction. James Pringle has reported on Asian affairs for more than forty years for The Times *in London, the* New York Times, *and Reuters.*

When I saw Comrade Duch sentenced to life in prison at the Khmer Rouge Tribunal here, it was like the end of a very weary story that began in April, 1979, when I was one of a group of six foreign journalists permitted to fly into Phnom

James Pringle, "The End of Duch," *Asia Sentinel*, February 10, 2012. Copyright © 2012 by Asia Sentinel. All rights reserved. Reproduced by permission.

Penh for a day after its liberation by the Vietnamese army on Jan. 7 of that year.

I seem to have been living with Duch, the 'revolutionary' name for former mathematics teacher Kaing Guek Eav, since the time 33 years ago when I found his picture on the floor of the former Tuol Sleng school, which had become S.21, the most notorious torture and interrogation center in the country, with congealed blood on the concrete, and a feeling as if the last desperate scream still hung in the air.

The whole awful place stank of death, fear and neglect, and when I went back some months later, I heard how in one terrible day 160 babies and children—the offspring of prisoners being tortured—had been flung from the third storey to their deaths on the concrete ground, because 'they were a nuisance.'

It was a picture of the then bat-eared Duch, with his wife and two children with other grinning torturers at Tuol Sleng, standing for a group portrait. I learned then that his family had come from the town of Stoung, north of the great Tonle Sap Lake. I also saw documents signed by Duch, including one giving the names and ages of a group of nine Khmer Rouge soldiers who arrived at S.21—the youngest was nine. "Eliminate every last one," Duch had scrawled in Khmer script.

A Chilling Visit

In Phnom Penh that day in 1979, I slipped away from an official reception and speech-making by the new Vietnamese-imposed regime meeting at the old French colonial HQ near the Tonle Sap river that joins with the Mekong here, and saw Cambodians in rags kneeling on the ground picking up individual grains of rice.

This pathetic group of skeletons smiled shyly at a couple of foreigners, before hauling themselves to their feet and tottering off, as if they felt their suffering was an eyesore for us, and they didn't want to bother our sensitivities with such a sight.

A few months later, People's Republic of Kampuchea officials gave me a visa for a longer stay, and I was driven with a few other journalists and government minders around the great Tonle Sap lake, staying the night in a deserted but famous Siem Reap hotel, said to be haunted because it had been a Khmer Rouge torture center, and seeing Angkor Wat with an armed escort of what were then known as 'Heng Samrin' troops.

Heng Samrin was a pint-sized commander and former Khmer Rouge who had joined the Vietnamese army, which had invaded Cambodia in December, 1978, and ousted Pol Pot and his dreadful cohorts. Comrade Duch, I learned at Tuol Sleng, was one of the last people to escape the city, seen by two of the seven survivors at S.21, out of 14,000 souls, spared by their skill in painting Pol Pot portraits, or repairing cars and other machinery.

In Stoung, I located Duch's family and spoke to his mother, who resembled her son down to her ears. She had not known Duch had two [children] now until I showed her the picture of her grandchildren at Tuol Sleng.

She recalled that under Khmer Rouge rule, the dutiful son had sent a Jeep to pick her up and take her to Phnom Penh for a brief visit. "I couldn't understand why the city was empty, and completely without power at night," the baffled woman told me.

It was not until 2006 that the Khmer Rouge Tribunal was established, and I saw Duch at last in court. He had remained at large for more than 20 years until he was found working for a Christian aid agency on the Thai-Cambodian border by the Irish photographer, Nic Dunlop, who always carried his picture (Duch may have had cosmetic surgery because his ears looked almost normal now). He was soon taken into custody by the regime of strongman prime minister Hun Sen, who had eased out Heng Samrin from the top job, and was ruling with an iron hand.

These days, visitors can see Hun Sen's portrait with national assembly president Hemg Samrin and senate president Chea Sim, both former Khmer Rouge, by this time forming a trium-virate with Hun Sen; their picture together is displayed in every

A memorial displays the skulls of victims at Choeung Ek, the best-known of the Killing Fields sites and where about seventeen thousand people were killed. © Shaul Schwarz/Getty Images News/Getty Images.

town and village, adapting Orwell's 'Big Brother' into the 'three Big Brothers.'

In late July, 2010, I watched the former commandant of Tuol Sleng sentenced to 35 years in prison for war crimes and crimes against humanity. He was, taking into account the time he'd already served and other considerations, likely to serve 19 years, which left the distinct possibility that he could live to see freedom again, and this brought chagrin to many.

It seemed, as people noted, too light a sentence for a man 'addicted to the sight of blood,' as one person described him in trial testimony. He admitted himself drawing blood from dozens of bodies, and killing people this way. The tortures at Tuol Sleng, including force-feeding prisoners human excrement, whipping, electric shocks, needles under fingernails and waterboarding, were methods taught to interrogators by Duch, who kept a notebook of torture methods. Later, in the nineties, he claimed to be 'born again' and earned a small Bible, which he may have carried into court last Friday.

A Record of Extreme Brutality

Under Duch's directions, ordinary Cambodians and foreign yachtsmen who had fallen into his hands while sailing off Cambodia, were bizarrely accused of working the CIA, KGB, British intelligence and Vietnamese security organs. Children taken to the Choeung Ek killing fields had their brains dashed out against a strong tree, while adult prisoners dug their own graves, then were hit on the back of the head with a hoe.

Then, last Friday, Duch received, on appeal, a life sentence, and last weekend Cambodia rejoiced that he would never walk out of prison alive. Duch reminds me of nothing so much as another example of the banality of evil. The idea of the banality of evil came originally from Hannah Arendt, in her 1963 work, 'Eichmann in Jerusalem' on the Nazi war criminal.

It described her thesis that the principal wrongs in history generally were not carried out by fanatics or sociopaths, but rather by ordinary people—and Duch was definitely ordinary.

Though three senior leaders of the Khmer Rouge remain to be tried, it seemed the horror of Cambodia that had lasted since the coup in March, 1970, that ousted then Prince Norodom Sihanouk, had a chance of coming to an end at last.

The Khmer Rouge killed those who spoke foreign languages, but they themselves had studied in Paris. Their revolution was a mixture of [French philosopher Jean-Jacques] Rousseau—man is born free but is everywhere in chains—Mao [Zedong, Chinese Communist dictator], Jacobin terror [during the revolution of 1789–1799], and [Soviet dictator Joseph] Stalin's kulak massacres in the Ukraine, and Hitler's persecution of Jews and Gypsies (in the Khmer Rouge case, the Muslim Cham minority and the Vietnamese residents of Cambodia, besides 'city people' from Phnom Penh, who were forced out in a massive evacuation on April 17th, 1975, one of history's most infamous deeds.

"The crimes committed by Kaing Guek Eav were undoubtedly among the worst in recorded human history," said Kong Srim, the presiding judge of the supreme court chambers.

Cambodians were still faced with unprecedented challenges in recovering from the tragedies caused by the crimes committed by Kaing Guek Eav, Kong Srim said.

The first time I saw Cambodia was during the American 'incursion' in May of 1970. Flying over the country then in a rickety South Vietnamese helicopter, I beheld a landscape pocked with craters, the result of the secret bombing that had been ordered by President Richard Nixon and his national security adviser, Henry Kissinger, in 1969.

Some commentators have wondered since just how much the American bombings, which killed tens of thousands of Cambodians before being stopped by Congress in 1973, had to do with the ferocity of the Khmer Rouge, under whose rule an estimated 1.7 million people were put to death or died of hunger or overwork.

In the countryside, on the second visit in 1979, I took a brief low-flying Russian helicopter ride over Battambang countryside and saw half-starved oxen pulling wooden carts along mine-laden and bomb-blasted roads; it seemed Cambodia had reverted to the 14th century CE; it looked like the Middle Ages.

In Phnom Penh, mountains of wrecked automobiles stood alongside piles of rusty refrigerators, unacceptable bourgeois toys in Pol Pot's 'Democratic Kampuchea.' I saw worthless currency blowing in the breeze outside the bombed-out national bank.

This week, US journalist Elizabeth Becker, one of the very few Western reporters to interview Pol Pot during Khmer Rouge in late 1978, said after the Duch life sentence that the Tribunal on the Khmer Rouge atrocities here had started what she happily called 'a Cambodian renaissance.'

Facing the Past

She told students in a lecture at Pannasastra University here: "Before the tribunal, history seemed off limits here, but now Cambodians are finding their voices, finding it is possible to start talking. The grief and trauma of the Khmer Rouge years are now legitimate and recognized, and the Cambodians are telling their stories."

She said there had been 30 years of silence on the horrors of the Khmer Rouge regime, and no official acknowledgement that a great crime had been committed. But, with the tribunal, the crime had been acknowledged.

She thought that it had taken the same amount of time for both Germans and the Japanese to come to terms with World War Two and its horrors.

(Just hours after the interview with Pol Pot, in that French colonial HQ mentioned earlier, the three person party, including American journalist Richard Dudman of the *St. Louis Post-Dispatch*, and British academic Malcolm Caldwell, one of the few Western supporters of the Pol Pot regime, was reduced to two, when Caldwell was shot to death in the guesthouse where they all stayed, probably slain because Caldwell may have shown some questioning of the Khmer Rouge line after seeing Democratic Kampuchea on the ground).

Meanwhile, the trials of the surviving leaders, most notably Brother Number Two Nuon Chea, 85, are under way.

Unlike Duch, who did show some token remorse for his unimaginably heinous crimes, they have not admitted their guilt, and seem to want to place the widespread killing at that time on the Vietnamese, whose army ultimately overturned the Pol Pot regime and, in the short term, rescued the ill and starving Cambodians.

Meanwhile, a defense lawyer for Nuon Chea this week quoted from an article containing allegations that National Assembly President Heng Samrin and Senate President Chea Sim may have committed serious crimes during the Khmer Rouge era.

Lawyer Jasper Pauw cited accusations from a 2005 article written by American academic Stephen Heder, a noted historian of the Khmer Rouge.

"Various evidence implicates Heng Samrin in war crimes—massacres of Vietnamese civilians—committed by troops under his command during cross-border raids into Vietnam in 1977, he said, quoting Heder's 2005 report.

Problems with War Crimes Trials

He then repeated allegations in the 37-page article by Heder that Chea Sim was responsible for killing evacuees and other people, reportedly based on Heder's interview with residents in the area.

This is just what Cambodia's strongman, prime minister Hun Sen, had feared might happen—allegations touching some of the top people of the current Cambodian government. Hun Sen is likely to be furious over this attack on his henchmen, and is quite capable of lashing out, diplomats say, as he has done often enough in the past.

Meanwhile, myriad other difficulties face the Tribunal. Despite tribunal costs of more than US$150 million, many of the 300 Cambodian staff have not been paid since last October, although some funds from Germany became available for some salary payments this week.

Meanwhile, a UN-appointed Swiss Judge, Laurent Kasper-Ansermet, has been prevented from assuming his official duties, accused of tweeting about genocide cases 003 and 004, with which the Phnom Penh government does not want to proceed.

The standoff over the appointment of Kasper-Ansermet has prompted some speculation the UN could withdraw from the proceedings before the completion of the trial of the three ageing Khmer Rouge leaders.

The US wishes the Swiss lawyer to continue with the prosecutions that include the Khmer Rouge's naval commander Mean Muth and Air Force Chief Sou Met, who are accused of responsibility for the deaths of tens of thousands of slave laborers during Khmer Rouge rule, particular over the building of a huge secret airport at Kompong Chhnang that the Chinese had shown interest in.

Kasper-Ansermet is unable to officially sit in the court, although he goes to the tribunal every day. He recently mentioned to journalists his time at the tribunal had been like 'walking in shackles.'

For his part, Hun Sen has demanded the tribunal undertake no new prosecutions, warning of civil war if more indictments are issued. The 'war' would start, presumably, with the former Khmer Rouge allies of these named.

"It's all potentially a big mess," said one court official, speaking on condition of anonymity. "It's difficult to see how this stand-off will be resolved."

For the present, Cambodians are just happy to have seen the execrable Duch put away for life.

CHAPTER 3

Personal Narratives

Chapter Exercises

1. Writing Prompt

Imagine that you are a teenager in Cambodia during the years of the Khmer Rouge regime. Not only have you been separated from your family and left unaware of what has happened to them, you have been placed in a labor camp and recruited to be a Khmer Rouge soldier. Write a one-page journal entry reflecting your thoughts.

2. Group Activity

Form into groups and come up with five interview questions that you might ask young people living in Khmer Rouge labor camps. The questions might concern whether your interviewees were evacuated from cities, where their families are, and whether they believe in the aims of the Khmer Rouge.

Past Still Haunts Khmer Genocide Survivor

Antonio Graceffo

In the following viewpoint, Matt Sindvith recounts his experiences as a survivor of the Cambodian genocide. He opens up about his life in Cambodia and in the United States to Antonio Graceffo, a Khmer-speaking freelance journalist he meets while driving his taxi in Washington, DC. Sindvith says that survivors of other atrocities have been able to put their struggles and pain behind them, but that he has not been able to come to terms with the horrors he experienced. The war and genocide in Cambodia robbed him of his country, his culture, and his beloved family members, he says. Graceffo is an American writer and adventurer fluent in several languages and currently living in Cambodia.

"I risked my life to get here, and I have done nothing with my time in America," says taxi driver Matt Sindvith. "I have seen women who were raped, or people who survived the war in Bosnia or Sarajevo. They were able to put that behind them. But I cannot. And, until I do, I can't get on with my life."

The generation of Khmers, aged twenty-five and over, share a history of survival, loss, and suffering. But for many, the trauma was never dealt with. And the scars of a war, which ended more than two decades ago, remain open wounds that prevent them from advancing.

Stuck in traffic on the Washington Beltway, I can only see the back of the driver's head, but the man in the photo on the license, which dangles from the sun visor, looks like a Khmer.

"*Sua Sedai*," I begin, going out on a limb. "*Da nyat junjet Khmer dey?*"

Slowly, he answers me, and we begin a rudimentary conversation. "I'm sorry," he says, switching to heavily accented English. "I have nearly lost my language." His tone of voice conveys his embarrassment.

By the time we reach my home, Matt has given me a brief summary of the events of his life. Not only had Pol Pot and the Khmer Rouge driven him from Cambodia, robbing him of his language, culture, and way of life, but they had also murdered both his mother and father.

"My dream, before I die," said Matt, "is to find my sister."

The last time Matt saw his younger sister, Sok Pola, was in 1980, when he escaped to a refugee camp in Thailand.

"A few years ago, I heard she was still alive," he told me. "A Khmer friend in America said that he had seen my sister working in a garment factory in either Sihanoukville or Koh Kong. I was told she is married." Matt trailed off. He radiated a sadness that was of an intensity I had never seen before. Thinking about his baby sister obviously filled him with deep emotions: loss, anger, and loneliness. In anyone else, tears might have come. But after getting to know Matt better, I would discover that he had moved beyond the stage of grief. Years of privation and hardship had drained him of his tears.

What are the odds that some strange Karmic force would bring together a Khmer-speaking journalist, just returned from Phnom Penh, and a Cambodian holocaust survivor, in need of a friend? Not quite believing that I was interested in helping him, Matt wrote out the names of his parents and siblings.

"I don't know how to write them in English," he told me.

"It's OK," I encouraged him. "Just write it in Khmer."

He paused again. "I almost don't remember how," he said. "Can you imagine not remembering how to write the names of your family members?"

Matt and I agreed to meet a few days later, and over a bowl of Burmese soup, the closest thing to Khmer food we could find in the District, he told me his story.

"I don't trust people," he began, "and I don't like to talk about those things." He meant the Pol Pot time.

It was obviously difficult for Matt to talk. Like so many Khmers, he has been walking around with the horrific story of his life bottled up inside of him. Under the best of circumstances, Khmer culture teaches that you are never supposed to talk about a problem. With reference to the Khmer Rouge regime, this policy becomes even more extreme. Having a selective memory and an absolute refusal to dredge up the past is the only way that victims and perpetrators are able to live side by side in modern Cambodia, without revenge killings happening every day.

Many people compare the Cambodian auto-genocide to the Holocaust of Jews under the Nazis. And, while there are many similarities, there are two fundamental differences that make it even harder for Khmers to let the past go. First of all, twenty percent of the Khmer population was murdered, not by an outside force, but by other Khmers. Second of all, not a single Khmer was excluded from participation in the genocide. Every single Khmer living in Cambodia between 1975 and 1979, was a victim, a perpetrator, or both.

Matt's father was a military officer under the French and under Prime Minister Prince Sihanouk. After he retired, he served as a high-ranking police official in the Lon Nol government.

"He received two pensions," said Matt proudly. "One from France and one from Cambodia."

In 1975, when the city fell to the Khmer Rouge, Matt's family was living in Tutapong, Phnom Penh. According to Matt, when the Khmer Rouge soldiers marched in, they gave everyone just twenty-four hours to evacuate the city.

We didn't want to leave," he said, "but they kicked us out."

As an observer to the aftermath of the Cambodian civil war, the question I always ask is, "Why didn't you escape to America in 1975?"

"In 1975 people didn't talk about escape. They were just happy the shooting had stopped. Also, we didn't want to leave Cambodia."

Matt is echoing the sentiments of most Khmers. Of all of the peoples I have met in my years of living abroad, I have never seen a people so completely bound to their homeland.

"Even in 1979, when the war was over, I didn't think of leaving the country. If I had wanted to leave I would have left in 1975. My family had money and connections. They tried to send me with an American evacuation, but I wouldn't go."

Matt's older brother and sister, who were already married, went off with their families.

"By chance, my whole family met up at a temple a few days later. It was the last time I saw most of them."

Matt's mother had wanted to go west, but his father wanted to go back to his homeland, of Kompong Cham.

"This was a mistake," said Matt. "Too many people knew my father there. And because he was a former soldier and a police officer, he was singled out."

Soon afterwards, the Khmer Rouge separated the children from the adults.

"I only saw my mother once more, in 1977."

The Khmer Rouge favored the country people, who they called Khmer Ja, or old people. Conversely, they hated the city people, who they called Khmer Tmai, or new people.

"We tried to hide the fact that we were from the city," said Matt. "But everything we did, we gave ourselves away. Even the way I talked, they knew I was a city boy.

"When they took my mother in 1977, my sister wanted to go with her. But I told her not to, or she would die also."

I asked Matt just how well the average Khmer understood the situation while it was happening.

"At the time I didn't understand anything; I only wanted to survive. The average person at the time didn't have a global understanding of what was happening. And we had no idea how bad the future would be. I had never considered running away to America. In fact, before 1979, I had barely even heard of America."

The entire population of Cambodia was organized into work groups and toiled at forced labor, constantly in fear of execution.

"It was like Auschwitz. We woke up at 6:00 A.M., no breakfast, and walked an hour to where we had to work. We worked 'til lunch and walked back. Lunch was a little bit of watery porridge. To supplement our diet, we ate anything we could find: water grass, stewed or steamed with salt. We ate too many strange things: grasshoppers, rats, lizards.

"My sister got more food, because she was a girl and younger. She tried to give it to me. But I wanted her to have it. After we ate, we walked back, and worked until six or seven. We ate dinner, another small bowl of porridge, then we had a criticism meeting. After that, we slept.

"At the meetings, I was always singled out and beaten because I was a city boy, and I could read, and speak French. A village boy used objects to beat me, but I didn't resist. It is good I didn't resist, because I would have been killed.

"I don't know how anyone could survive. American kids in general would die.

"When you were sick, you would tell them, but there was no medicine. Don't be a lazy bastard, they would say, get back to work. Your illnesses were never treated.

"Pol Pot was not well-known at that time. When I was in the city, we never knew that name. We knew the name Ieng Saray, but not Pol Pot. He was like a godfather, the man behind the scenes.

"The name we heard every day was *Angka* (organization). When they wanted you to do something, they always said, *Angka* wants you to do this or that. And if you didn't do it, you were betraying the party, *Angka*, not the individual.

"*Angka* was a faceless organization who issued all the laws and edicts. Who were they referring to? It could be some idiot over there who made up his own rules."

In the final year of the regime, *Angka* began feeding on itself. Paranoia in higher echelons caused major purges, resulting in the execution of thousands of Khmer Rouge cadre.

"Hun Sen ran to Vietnam to avoid being killed," said Matt, referring to the current Prime Minister. "Hun Sen pretended to be the savior of Cambodia. He led the Vietnamese troops into Cambodia, ending the Khmer Rouge regime.

"I think there must have been some kind of deal there.

"Vietnamese soldiers got no pay or food from their government. They had to steal from the people. The Vietnamese soldiers randomly killed people.

"My sister knew a teacher who survived, and he took us into his house. He was the mayor of the province, appointed by Hun Sen. But, when some guerillas were killed by the Vietnamese, the mayor was accused of collaboration, and he was killed. So, we lost our place to live."

His siblings went to the coast to look for work in a factory, and were recruited into Hun Sen's army, under Vietnamese control.

"They were rounding up Khmer Rouge and killing them. You think you would want revenge for what had happened. But even when I had a gun in my hand, I couldn't kill the Khmer Rouge. I was not a murderer."

The only hint at vengeance Matt ever made was: "If I had money and time I want to find out who killed my parents.

"My younger brother was very street smart, much more than me. If I had to live in the ghetto or hustle, I would never survive. He went with the Vietnamese army and he was happy.

"The commander liked me and trusted me not to run away. The next day, we were supposed to go on a large offensive, and I ran to Thailand. Two other boys went with me, but they turned back. Most likely, they were arrested and killed."

In a camp in Thailand, he began doing volunteer work for aid organizations. Originally, he had been planning to go back to Cambodia, join the Khmer Serey, and fight against the Vietnamese occupation.

"But working for the aid organizations opened my mind. I realized I had been living in a tiny fish bowl. And I never wanted to live like that again."

Matt began writing random letters to people in the West, asking them to sponsor him for immigration. One day, he got a response from a judge in North Dakota.

"The judge was Jewish, a survivor of the Holocaust, so he was very interested in helping me.

"I remember it vividly, when he picked me up at the airport. It was a completely different world.

There was a blizzard when I arrived. It was the first time I ever saw snow."

One of the psychological impacts of the trauma that Matt, and other refugees, experience is that he tries to cut all of his ties with the past.

"I lost contact with the judge. He is most likely dead now, because [he] would be very old."

Matt found it impossible to live in North Dakota. On the recommendation of some Khmer friends, he moved to Maryland, and lived in a home with several other refugees. He finished high school, graduated from a college, and then studied at George Mason University, majoring in engineering.

Matt was on his way to becoming one of the major success stories for the Khmer community when suddenly, in his final semester of school, his years of suffering caught up with him.

"I just snapped," he said. "I quit university. My father had been a devout Buddhist, but I stopped going to temple. I broke off with all of my friends and I didn't want to know anyone."

Matt went from job to job, working in restaurants, doing security, and driving taxis, never getting close to anyone. Obviously desperate for a family, he said, "The judge was like a father to me," and, "the military commander was like a family to me," and, "the people I lived with in Maryland were like a family to me."

But he broke his ties with all of them.

As we talked, I felt honored that Matt trusted me enough to open up and share his story. At the same time, I felt he probably needed to talk. And I wondered how many Khmers must be walking around with some type of post-traumatic stress disorder and desperately in need of counseling, which their cultural norms would prevent them from seeking out.

At age forty-one, Matt is still single, with no marriage in sight. "I can't even deal with myself. I take life too seriously. I see a lot of sadness.

"I cherish where I come from," said Matt, "but I have tried to distance myself from anything that reminds me of the Khmer Rouge time. I tried to watch the film, *The Killing Fields*, but I couldn't. I lived through it—why did I need to watch the movie?

"Right now, I can't believe that for twenty years I had little or no contact with my people. I even lost my language. When I meet old people, I don't remember how to communicate with them. You have to address them a certain way, according to age and class, to show respect." He shook his head. "You speak Khmer better than me. I thought that could never happen. I was so good before.

"I used to write well," he continued. "Now I struggle to write the names of my family members. If I found them I would enlist a translator to communicate with them."

He kept asking me about modern Cambodia, and would shake his head remorsefully when I told him about the lawlessness, low levels of education, joblessness, and lack of hope.

"They were born in a period of time when they experienced no normalcy and no stability."

Matt had this to say about the proposed Khmer Rouge tribunals: "The trial is a travesty and a waste of time. By the time they start, these people will all be dead. And the ones who are alive show no remorse. Hun Sen hasn't pushed for the trial, maybe because he is one of them.

"We lost too much—everything. Sometimes I dream about helping the Cambodians, but I have nothing to offer. I know what it is like to be destitute and hopeless; I struggle with my own conflict. Those people right now need so much help. It's not a good feeling.

"I feel I failed myself. Earlier, all my friends expected me to do so well. When you lose your culture, it is hard to restore your pride. They all expected me to do well. The best student in my group, I quit the university and ties with all my old friends."

Matt's life is a lonely one.

"At home I only did homework, play chess, and read books. My parents didn't want me to play or ride a bicycle. I never had any exposure to the real world. So, now I have no social skills. I live with a Philippine family who treat me like a son. They want me to go out and socialize, but I don't want to.

"In this country, when you meet people, they ask, what do you do for a living? I am shy. I don't want to say I am only a taxi driver. If they gave me an hour to tell my story, I could explain what I have been through."

"But, they never give you an hour," I said.

"In 1975, we had burned all of our other photos so that the Khmer Rouge wouldn't discover my father in uniform. Only one photo of my mother survived. My sister carried it, secretly, and kept it safe from 1975 to 1979. She gave me that picture when I left for Thailand, and I have always carried it with me, thinking my mother would protect me.

"If my parents had lived, I would have been motivated to succeed. But now I have no reason to push myself. I have no family, no one to care for me.

"We think, why me? But the same thing happened in Rwanda and Bosnia. I have to let it go. I can't move on in my life 'til I let it go."

Khmer Rouge Survivor Describes Torture at S-21

Sopheng Cheang

The following viewpoint is a news story describing the testimony of Chum Mey as he recalls the torture and pain he endured at the Khmer Rouge's main torture center. He spoke in June 2009 as a witness in the UN war crimes trial of Kaing Guek Eav, or "Duch," the commander of the notorious S-21. Mey cries at any mention of the events because it reminds him of his wife and baby, both of whom were killed during the Cambodian genocide. The relentless torture Mey endured at S-21 caused him to falsely confess to accusations that fit the regime's radical Communist perspective. Sopheng Cheang is a writer for the Associated Press.

One of three living survivors from the Khmer Rouge's main torture center testified Tuesday that he endured beatings, electric shocks and had his toenails pulled out but was spared execution because he knew how to fix cars.

Weeping as he spoke, 79-year-old Chum Mey said he cries every night and any mention of the Khmer Rouge reminds him of his wife and baby—both killed under the regime whose 1970s rule of Cambodia left an estimated 1.7 million people dead.

Three decades after the fall of the Khmer Rouge, a U.N.-backed tribunal is piecing together Cambodia's dark past with the trial of Kaing Guek Eav—better known as Duch—who headed the S-21 prison in Phnom Penh between 1975 and 1979.

Duch sat impassively and listened as Chum Mey spoke.

"I was beaten for 12 days and nights. I was beaten day and night. I could hardly walk," said Chum Mey, who was arrested in early 1975 and remained jailed until Vietnamese troops ousted the Khmer Rouge regime and liberated the prison inmates in January 1979.

First he was hit with sticks, then subjected to a week of torture with live electrical wires.

Like most prisoners at S-21, Chum Mey was forced to make confessions that suited the regime's radical communist perspective. Although most apparently were innocent, many confessed to being spies for the CIA, Russia's KGB or Vietnam.

"I kept responding that I didn't know anything about the CIA and KGB, but they used pliers and twisted off my toenail," he said. After extracting one big toenail, torturers shifted to the other foot. "They tried to twist the other one off with the pliers but the nail didn't come out so they pulled it out with their hands."

"I confessed that I had joined the CIA and KGB but it was a lie. I said it because I was so badly beaten," he said.

Chum Mey turned to Duch at one point and asked him angrily why prisoners were accused of working for the CIA.

Duch remained silent until a judge ordered him to speak. The 66-year-old calmly answered that the term CIA was used to refer to anyone who opposed the Khmer Rouge—but it didn't necessarily have anything to do with the U.S. Central Intelligence Agency.

"The real CIA is different from people accused by the regime of being CIA," Duch said. "You were identified as someone who opposed the regime, that's why we called you CIA."

Some 16,000 men, women and children were detained and tortured at S-21 before being sent for execution at the "Killing

Fields" on the outskirts of the capital where thousands were killed and their bodies dumped. Chum Mey is thought to be one of only seven survivors, and one of three still alive today.

Chum Mey's torture stopped once his captors realized he had a useful skill. He was put to work fixing his jailers' cars, tractors, sewing machines and typewriters.

"When I was tortured, I no longer felt like a human being. I felt like an animal," he said. Prisoners were kept shackled in cramped cells, and ate, slept and relieved themselves in the same spot.

A fellow survivor, Vann Nath, 63, testified Monday that he ate his meager meals—three teaspoons of porridge twice a day— next to corpses and was so hungry that he considered eating human flesh. Vann Nath escaped execution because he was an artist who took the job of painting portraits of the Khmer Rouge's late leader, Pol Pot.

Duch is the first senior Khmer Rouge figure to face trial and the only one to acknowledge responsibility for his actions. Senior leaders Khieu Samphan, Nuon Chea, Ieng Sary and Ieng Sary's wife, Ieng Thirith, are all detained and likely to face trial in the next year or two.

Duch (pronounced Doik) has previously testified that being sent to S-21 was tantamount to a death sentence and that he was only following orders to save his own life. He is charged with crimes against humanity, war crimes and murder.

A Cambodian Labor Camp Inmate Is Reunited with His Brother

Daran Kravanh and Bree Lafreniere

The following viewpoint details the experience of Daran Kravanh, who survived a Khmer Rouge work camp during the years of the Cambodian genocide. Kravanh recalls an unexpected meeting with his brother. Together, the two made plans to try to escape to Thailand, plans which were never carried out. Kravanh made it to the United States as a refugee in 1988 and is now a social worker and activist in the state of Washington. Bree Lafreniere is the author of Music Through the Dark: A Tale of Survival in Cambodia.

As the Khmer Rouge regime went on, life became more and more difficult. The killing and terror never stopped. There was never enough food, enough freedom, enough joy. The other April 17 [1975, the day the Khmer Rouge took control of Phnom Penh, the Cambodian capital] people were so vulnerable to illness that there were many outbreaks of malaria, cholera, and other diseases. When I got malaria, I became so ill I could not work and was taken to the village to rest. While burning with a high fever and mad with headache, I saw my brother Chamroeun once again.

Bree Lafreniere, "Chapter 7: Reconciliation," *Music Through the Dark: A Tale of Survival in Cambodia*. Honolulu: University of Hawai'i Press, 2000, pp. 137–142. Copyright © 2000 by Bree Lafreniere. All rights reserved. Reproduced by permission.

An Unexpected Meeting

Lying on my stomach on the floor of the kitchen building, I looked up to see a figure walking toward me from fifty meters away. He looked like my brother Chamroeun. I thought I was dreaming or confused from my fever. I closed my eyes and opened them again. It was Chamroeun. He was very thin and small and he was crying and mucus ran out of his nose. He looked like a child, but I knew it was him because he was wearing the shorts my mother had made for him from the same material she had used for mine.

"Chamroeun!" I called. I pushed the blanket from my body and ran to him. "Where have you been?" I asked him.

"I've been in the forest," he said.

"Where are our parents?" I asked, forgetting they were dead.

"Oh, little brother, don't think about that now."

"What has happened to Cambodia?" I cried.

"Hush now, brother, and lie back down."

Chamroeun came close to me. At first we didn't know what to say to each other. Quietly he began to sing forbidden songs in my ears. "Do you remember these songs?"

I smiled. "Yes, yes. I remember."

Even though we were grown men, we slept together that night holding each other. In the morning I woke and looked at my brother's sleeping body. He was still wearing the necklace my father had given him. It was a small Buddha inside a box on a silver chain. My father had given it to Chamroeun to protect him from harm. I thought of my father and my mind filled with memories of our family.

I was overjoyed to see my brother again. And as I hugged him again, I heard the sounds of his empty stomach. "Brother, you are so thin. I must get something for you to eat," I said. I went to dig up a potato and pick an ear of corn I had grown myself. I returned to my brother and watched him eat the corn. I remember his face so clearly: the kernels of corn around his mouth mixed with the tears from his eyes; the sadness of his stories mixed with his gladness at finding me. My brother was so thin but so beautiful. So beautiful! You cannot imagine.

We began to talk. I learned that Chamroeun had been looking for me for a long time. After the last time I saw him, he had returned to his wife and children. He had then run away in April 1975 when he found out the Khmer Rouge were planning to kill him. He hid in the forest for many months and tried, as I did, to escape to Thailand, but he was unable to leave. He decided he would have to find a way to live in Cambodia under the Khmer Rouge.

Because of his experience being held hostage by the Khmer Rouge in 1971, he knew that paper and pen alone would ensure his survival in the new society. He left the forest, found paper and pen, and wrote out a permit in small print so neat it looked like it had been typewritten. It said something like: "Allow Kong Chamroeun to live and eat in your cooperative." So he traveled from cooperative to cooperative looking for our family. Chamroeun talked with sorrow about his wife Sophat, his son Tito, and his little daughters. The Khmer Rouge had already killed his daughters. He didn't know where his wife and son were.

Family Memories

While Chamroeun was talking, a woman suddenly appeared at the door with a soldier behind her. She pointed at me. "He is the one who took the corn!" I was scared but Chamroeun was calm and said to the soldier, "I have permission to eat here." He showed the soldier the paper. The soldier looked at it for a long time. "Okay. He can eat the corn."

Chamroeun told me he had met his old employee, Mr. Chhien, and that it was he who had told him where to find me. Mr. Chhien was then a section leader in a cooperative nearby. Chamroeun told me he would go to live with him and some of the Khmer Rouge soldiers. I did not like the idea of my brother living with the Khmer Rouge, but he believed no harm would

Many urban Cambodians were forced by the Khmer Rouge to relocate to communal farms such as this one, pictured in 1978. © AP Images/Elizabeth Becker.

come to him. Indeed, he thought it would be safer for him. I didn't want him to leave, but he left with a promise to return.

About five days later, he stood outside my hut and called to me, "Tooch! Tooch!" I had nearly forgotten my old nickname and smiled at the sound of it. I let my brother in and he gave me some palm sugar and tobacco. He told me he was living in the Leach district with the Khmer Rouge. "What do you do over there?" I asked him.

"I am a doctor," he said.

"How can you be a doctor?"

"I assisted the doctor who stayed with us when we were young, do you remember? That's all the training the Khmer Rouge require."

"Chamroeun! How can you live with the Khmer Rouge? That is like living with a sharp knife. You must be very careful."

Chamroeun spent the night with me. After that he visited me every few days. He walked across the forest at night and brought me sugar and other bits of food. He fed me like he was my mother and father. Once he took me to his hut. I saw his change of clothes hanging on the wall and the folding cot he slept on. "Look at this," he said to me. He removed the scarf from around his neck and unrolled it. The outline of our parents' feet was drawn on the scarf. "I wear this to feel them close to me," he said.

Once Chamroeun took me to the kitchen in his cooperative. "You can eat as much rice as you want," he whispered. But I could hardly eat because I knew it was food that was intended for someone as hungry as I. Chamroeun saw my hesitation, but he had a different idea. He looked into my eyes and spoke in a firm voice. "You eat this food. Just think of yourself, Daran. If you are going to die, you must have a reason to die, not just some little mistake. I will never die. I will always stay with you. I don't want you to die, so eat this food." Even in the Khmer Rouge time, when it wasn't easy to think, my brother was bright, especially about complicated things. It made no difference whether you thought of anything useful. It was of no consequence. You could use your mind to solve mathematical problems or questions of physics, but you could not solve the human problems or use your mind to end your suffering or that of those around you.

Hoping to Escape

Yes, my brother was bright. But in the end even his brightness could not save him. I do not want to say what happened to him, the words are so bitter in my mouth.

Chamroeun told me he wanted to escape to Thailand. I argued with him and told him of my troubles in trying to cross the border, but in his desperation he would not listen to me. "It is just a matter of time before someone finds out we are brothers and we are educated," he said. "Do you think your accordion will always save you? We have no choice but to go."

We made a plan to meet on a particular night at the hut of Mr. Phat, one of the low-level leaders of the cooperative. I waited for my brother all night and grew more anxious with each hour that passed. At about 4:30 in the morning, I heard Chamroeun's voice. "I am sorry, Tooch. I couldn't come sooner. There were a lot of soldiers cleaning the forest." "Cleaning the forest" meant they were looking for people trying to escape. We decided to try again in a few days.

I waited and waited for Chamroeun's return, but he did not come for me. I needed to know what was wrong. After several days I borrowed a bicycle from Mr. Chhoeun and took a bag of oranges and went to Chamroeun's hut. When I arrived I did not see him. I saw a Khmer Rouge named Chon with whom Chamroeun had been living. "Where is Chamroeun?" I asked him.

"I don't know," he said.

I knew I should not ask questions but I needed to see Chamroeun. So I asked him again, "How can you live with Chamroeun and not know where he is?"

The man grew irritated and yelled at me, "He was sent away to cut bamboo."

I looked around and saw Chamroeun's scarf still hanging on the wall. I knew he would not go anywhere without it. Then . . . oh this image makes me cry . . . I looked under the cot where my brother slept and saw a small pool of blood. Then I saw blood splattered on the walls. I knew it was my brother's blood, and I felt sick, my heart frantic. I felt faint. I felt I might die. I looked at the man and knew he had killed my brother but I said nothing. I was scared then that he would kill me too and for a few moments I did not care. But something pushed me out of the hut.

I rode the bicycle along the dirt road and cried out for my brother's soul. I shouted his name over and over. Dust blew up into my face and mixed with my tears. When I returned to my hut, I put the oranges intended for my brother on a plate. I thought of my brother's talents, his beauty and compassion, his desire for life and justice. Finally I said a long prayer for him and wished him well in the next life. I left the oranges on that plate until they lost their glow and became rotten. Then I took them to the rice field where I buried them.

When I returned to my cooperative, my section leader said, "Where have you been?" I told him I had malaria and had stayed home to rest. He said he would ask Mr. Phat about that. He then summoned Mr. Phat and asked him why I had been absent. Mr. Phat was nervous. I prayed he would lie for me. "He was not feeling well," Mr. Phat said.

I was allowed to go. Down the road Mr. Phat looked at me with a long face and said, "If you were anyone else, today you would die."

I went back to work in the rice field. It was my assignment to take a string and measure out rows for the seedlings. That was an easy assignment for me. I had good eyesight and my mother had taught me how to measure land perfectly.

This work required that I look off into the distance. I held one end of the string while another man held the other end. As I looked at the horizon and the setting sun, Chamroeun's song about not knowing the future and not being able to reach the horizon returned to me. I sang that song quietly to myself and cried for my brother. I thought that my sorrow would surely kill me, but the comfort of death was still not to be mine.

Glossary

Angka A term used to refer to the Khmer Rouge leadership and ideology. Also spelled Angkar or Angkah.

Angkor Wat A large temple complex in northeastern Cambodia and the most famous of the country's ancient monuments.

Base People The Khmer Rouge term for the people under their control before their takeover of Cambodia was completed in 1975. Most were rural people.

Brother Number One The term for Khmer Rouge leader Pol Pot, which was intended to imply equality.

cadre A Khmer Rouge official.

Chams A Muslim minority living mostly in eastern Cambodia.

Choeung Ek A killing field outside Phnom Penh where many who were tortured at S-21 were eventually taken for execution.

Democratic People's Republic of Kampuchea Cambodia's name during the Khmer Rouge regime; often shortened to DPRK or PRK.

FUNCINPEC A Cambodian royalist party advocating the power of the monarchy. It stands for the French "Front Uni National pour un Cambodge Indépendant, Neutre, Pacifique, Et Coopératif," or National United Front for an Independent, Neutral, Peaceful, and Cooperative Cambodia. It was one of a number of factions struggling against the Khmer Rouge in the 1980s.

Indochina Older term for what are now the nations of Laos, Cambodia, and Vietnam. Mostly used during the French colonial era from the mid-1800s to the mid-1900s.

Kampuchea Another common name for Cambodia.

Kampuchea Krom Southeastern Cambodia along the Mekong River, where the population is split among Khmer and Vietnamese.

Khmer A Cambodian ethnicity and language.

Khmer Rouge "Red Khmer," a name given to Cambodia's radical Communist insurgency by King Sihanouk in the 1960s.

killing fields The areas where the Khmer Rouge killed and left behind the bodies of its victims.

Krama A checked scarf worn by Cambodian peasants and formerly a symbol of the Khmer Rouge. Also spelled Chroma or Kroma.

Mekong River A major Asian river that flows from China southeastward through to the South China Sea. It is the heart of Cambodia's rural life.

new people The Khmer Rouge term for city dwellers, merchants, and the educated; these were people intended for a lower position in their regime.

old people The Khmer Rouge term for the poor peasants of the countryside who were favored by the regime.

Phnom Penh The capital of Cambodia.

S-21 Security Prison 21, also known as Tuol Sleng. A former Phnom Penh high school that was turned into a torture and killing center by the Khmer Rouge and is now a memorial.

Santebal The Khmer Rouge secret police.

Tonle Sap An inland sea that forms part of the Mekong River in central Cambodia.

UNTAC The United Nations Transitional Authority in Cambodia, formed in 1992 to help guide the transition to peace after the departure of Vietnamese troops.

Vietnam War The conflict between North Vietnamese Communists trying to unify their country and US and South Vietnamese forces trying to stop the spread of communism. The war lasted from 1965 to 1975 and spilled into Cambodia in 1970.

Year Zero The beginning of the new era for Cambodia starting in 1975, according to the Khmer Rouge.

Organizations to Contact

The editors have compiled the following list of organizations concerned with the issues debated in this book. The descriptions are derived from materials provided by the organizations. All have publications or information available for interested readers. The list was compiled on the date of publication of the present volume; the information provided here may change. Be aware that many organizations take several weeks or longer to respond to inquiries, so allow as much time as possible.

Amnesty International
5 Penn Plaza, 14th Floor
New York, NY, 10001
(212) 807-8400 • fax: (212) 463-9193
e-mail: aimember@aiusa.org
website: www.amnestyusa.org

Amnesty International is a worldwide movement of people who campaign for internationally recognized human rights. Its vision is of a world in which every person enjoys all of the human rights enshrined in the Universal Declaration of Human Rights and other international human rights standards. Each year it publishes a report on its work and human rights concerns throughout the world.

Build Cambodia
1555 N. Astor, #45 West
Chicago, IL 60610
(312) 423-6689
e-mail: info@buildcambodia.org
website: www.buildcambodia.org

Build Cambodia is a US-based not-for-profit organization dedicated to helping Cambodians. The organization advocates for

Cambodian organizations in the United States, facilitates individual projects that Americans are undertaking, and leads regular fact-finding trips where committed adults tour Cambodia and visit unique places that few foreigners ever see. Its goal is to provide a steady flow of attention and resources for worthwhile efforts in Cambodia.

Cambodian Association of America (CAA)
2390 Pacific Ave.
Long Beach, CA 90806
(562) 988-1623
website: www.cambodianusa.com

CAA, incorporated as a nonprofit organization in 1975, is the oldest and largest Cambodian organization in the United States. The mission of the early founders was to assist Cambodian refugees in Southern California in acculturating to life in the United States, while preserving their Cambodian culture, customs, and values. The organization now provides services and programs that reach more than fifteen thousand people per year.

Human Rights Watch
350 Fifth Ave., 34th Floor
New York, NY 10118-3299
(212) 290-4700 • fax: (212) 736-1300
e-mail: hrwnyc@hrw.org
website: www.hrw.org

Founded in 1978, this nongovernmental organization conducts systematic investigations of human rights abuses in countries around the world. It publishes numerous books and reports on specific countries and issues as well as annual reports. Its website includes various discussions concerning human rights and international justice issues.

Montreal Institute for Genocide and Human Rights Studies (MIGS)
Concordia University
1455 De Maisonneuve Boulevard West
Montreal, Quebec, H3G 1M8 Canada
(514) 848-2424 ext. 5729 or 2404 • fax: (514) 848-4538
website: http://migs.concordia.ca

MIGS, founded in 1986, monitors for early warning signs of genocide in countries deemed to be at risk of mass atrocities. The institute houses the Will to Intervene (W2I) Project, a research initiative focused on the prevention of genocide and other mass atrocity crimes. The institute also collects and disseminates research on the historical origins of mass killings and provides comprehensive links to this and other research materials on its website.

STAND/United to End Genocide
1025 Connecticut Ave., Suite 310
Washington, DC 20036
(202) 556-2100
e-mail: info@standnow.org
website: www.standnow.org

STAND is the student-led division of United to End Genocide (formerly Genocide Intervention Network). STAND envisions a world in which the global community is willing and able to protect civilians from genocide and mass atrocities. In order to empower individuals and communities with the tools to prevent and stop genocide, STAND recommends activities from engaging government representatives to hosting fundraisers, and has more than one thousand student chapters at colleges and high schools.

United Human Rights Council (UHRC)
104 N. Belmont Street, Suite 313

Glendale, CA 91206
(818) 507-1933
website: www.unitedhumanrights.org

The United Human Rights Council is a committee of the Armenian Youth Federation. By means of action on a grassroots level the UHRC works toward exposing and correcting human rights violations of governments worldwide. The UHRC campaigns against violators in an effort to generate awareness through boycotts, community outreach, and education. The UHRC website focuses on the genocides of the twentieth century.

Youth Star Cambodia
PO Box 171
#17A, Street 598
Khan Tuol Kork Sangkat Boeung Kak 2
Phnom Penh, Cambodia
website: www.youthstarcambodia.org

Youth Star Cambodia's mission is to build a just and peaceful nation through citizen service, civic leadership, and social entrepreneurship. Youth Star recruits, trains, and coaches volunteer Cambodian university graduates for twelve to eighteen months of service in underserved rural communities where they work in education and youth development, health education, rural livelihoods/income generation, or good governance.

List of Primary Source Documents

The editors have compiled the following list of documents that either broadly address genocide and persecution or more narrowly focus on the topic of this volume. The full text of these documents is available from multiple sources in print and online.

Agreement Between the United Nations and the Royal Government of Cambodia Concerning the Prosecution of Crimes Committed During Democratic Kampuchea Era, June 6, 2003

A statement of principles on how trials of accused Khmer Rouge leaders should be conducted under both UN guidelines and Cambodian law. The principles remain controversial though trials continue into the second decade of the twenty-first century.

Bangkok Declaration, 1993

Asian nations declare their support for international agreements and standards for human rights while recognizing the need for the sovereignty and distinct values of independent states.

UN Convention Against Torture and Other Cruel, Inhuman, or Degrading Punishment, 1974

A draft resolution adopted by the United Nations General Assembly in 1974 opposing any nation's use of torture, unusually harsh punishment, and unfair imprisonment.

UN Convention on the Prevention and Punishment of the Crime of Genocide, December 9, 1948

A resolution of the United Nations General Assembly that defines genocide in legal terms and advises participating countries to prevent and punish actions of genocide in war and peacetime.

Decree Law No. 1: Establishment of People's Revolutionary Tribunal at Phnom Penh to Try the Pol Pot-Ieng Sary Clique for the Crime of Genocide, People's Revolutionary Council of Cambodia, July 15, 1979

After the Khmer Rouge was ousted by a Vietnamese invasion, the Vietnamese-supported People's Revolutionary Council pledged to hold Khmer Rouge leaders responsible for their crimes under the UN Genocide Convention.

Principles of International Law Recognized in the Charter of the Nuremburg Tribunal, United Nations International Law Commission, 1950

After World War II (1939–1945) the victorious allies legally tried surviving leaders of Nazi Germany in the German city of Nuremburg. The proceedings established standards for international law that were affirmed by the United Nations and by later court tests. Among other standards, national leaders can be held responsible for crimes against humanity, which might include "murder, extermination, deportation, enslavement, and other inhuman acts."

Report of the Group of United Nations Experts on Cambodia, March 15, 1999

As the last Khmer Rouge leaders surrendered and the group disbanded, the United Nations sent a group to Cambodia. Their report touched on the status of the country and the need to hold responsible those who committed atrocities.

United Nations Transitional Authority in Cambodia: Human Rights Component Final Report, September 1993

After the last Vietnamese troops left Cambodia, the United Nations Transitional Authority was sent in to help provide a transition to peace and stability. Upon its departure in 1993, it submitted a report to the United Nations on human rights conditions in the country.

Rome Statute of the International Criminal Court, July 17, 1998

This treaty created the International Criminal Court. It establishes the court's functions, jurisdiction, and structure.

United Nations General Assembly Resolution 96 on the Crime of Genocide, December 11, 1946

A resolution of the United Nations General Assembly that affirms genocide is a crime under international law.

Universal Declaration of Human Rights, United Nations, 1948

Soon after its founding, the United Nations approved this general statement of individual rights it hoped would apply to citizens of all nations.

Whitaker Report on Genocide, 1985

This report addresses the question of the prevention and punishment of the crime of genocide. It calls for the establishment of an international criminal court and a system of universal jurisdiction to ensure that genocide is punished.

For Further Research

Books

Var Hong Ashe, *From Phnom Penh to Paradise: Escape from Cambodia*. London: Hodder and Stoughton, 1988.

Elizabeth Becker, *When the War Was Over: The Voices of Cambodia's Revolution and Its People*. New York: Simon and Schuster, 1986.

Francois Bizot, *The Gate*. New York: Knopf, 2000.

Nayan Chanda, *Brother Enemy: The War After the War, A History of Indochina Since the Fall of Saigon*. New York: Harcourt Brace Jovanovich, 1986.

David P. Chandler, *A History of Cambodia*. Boulder, CO: Westview Press, 2008.

David P. Chandler and Ben Kiernan, eds., *Revolution and Its Aftermath in Kampuchea: Eight Essays*. New Haven, CT: Yale University Southeast Asia Studies Council, 1983.

Wilfred P. Deac, *Road to the Killing Fields: The Cambodian War of 1970–1975*. College Station: Texas A&M University Press, 1997.

David W.P. Elliott, ed., *The Third Indochina Conflict*. Boulder, CO: Westview Press, 1981.

Martin Stuart Fox and Bun Heang Ung, *The Murderous Revolution: Life and Death in Pol Pot's Kampuchea*. Sydney: APCOL, 1985.

Karl Jackson, ed., *Cambodia 1975–1978: Rendezvous with Death*. Princeton, NJ: Princeton University Press, 1989.

Ben Kiernan, *The Pol Pot Regime: Race, Power, and Genocide in the Cambodia Under the Khmer Rouge, 1975–79*. 3rd ed. New Haven, CT: Yale University Press, 2008.

Someth May, *Cambodian Witness: The Autobiography of Someth May*. London: Faber and Faber, 1986.

William Shawcross, *Cambodia's New Deal Contemporary Issues paper no. 1*. Washington, DC: Carnegie Endowment for International Peace, 1994.

Michael Vickery, *Cambodia 1975–1982*. Boston: South End, 1984.

Pin Yathay with John Man, *Stay Alive My Son*. New York: The Free Press, 1987.

Marilyn Young, *The Vietnam Wars: 1945–1990*. New York: Harper Perennial, 2001.

Periodicals and Internet Sources

Christiane Amanpour, "Survivor Recalls Horror of Cambodia Genocide," CNN World, April 7, 2008.

Associated Press, "A Key Monument to Horror Is Laid to Rest in Cambodia," *Los Angeles Times*, March 11, 2002.

"Baker's About Face on Cambodia," *Newsweek*, July 29, 1990.

BBC News, "Cambodia's Brutal Khmer Rouge Regime," September 19, 2007.

Christopher Hudson, "Beyond the Killing Fields," *Telegraph* (UK), March 16, 2012.

CNN World, "Cambodia's Pol Pot Reported Dead," April 15, 1998.

Guy DeLauney, "Life Term for Cambodia Khmer Rouge Jailer Duch," BBC News, February 3, 2012.

Dan Fletcher, "The Khmer Rouge," *Time*, February 17, 2009.

Kate Hodal, "Journalist Seeking Truth About Khmer Rouge 'Fears for His Life,'" *Guardian* (UK), March 25, 2012.

Zoltan Istvan, "Killing Fields Lure Tourists in Cambodia," *National Geographic*, January 10, 2003.

Joyce Koh, "Cambodia Embracing Capitalism with First IPO Since Pol Pot," Bloomberg, March 19, 2012.

Taylor Owen and Ben Kiernan, "Bombs over Cambodia: New Information Reveals That Cambodia Was Bombed Far More Heavily than Previously Revealed," *The Walrus*, October, 2006.

Jarrett Murphy, "Remembering the Killing Fields," CBS News, February 11, 2009.

Kong Sothanarith, "Departing Tribunal Judge Calls Two More Suspects 'Most Responsible,'" Voice of America News, May 3, 2012.

Nate Thayer, "Day of Reckoning," *Far Eastern Economic Review*, October 30, 1997.

Websites

Cambodian Genocide Program (www.yale.edu/cgp) Connected to Yale University's Southeast Asia Studies program, this website is the chief scholarly resource on the Cambodian genocide. It contains links to articles, original documents, maps, and photographs.

Cambodia Tribunal Monitor (www.cambodiatribunal.org) This website is maintained by a consortium of academic, philanthropic, and nonprofit organizations committed to providing public access to the process of bringing the Khmer Rouge to justice.

Digital Archive of Cambodian Holocaust Survivors (www.cybercambodia.com) This is a website maintained by survivors of the Cambodian genocide. It contains links to the stories of survivors, photographs of victims, and information on modern Cambodia.

Film

Enemies of the People (2009) This documentary follows the journey of Cambodian genocide survivor Thet Sambath, as he seeks confessions from Khmer Rouge perpetrators.

The Killing Fields (1984) This film is based on the true story of the friendship between Sydney Schanberg, a reporter for the *New York Times,* and Dith Pran, his translator and assistant.

The Last Word: Dith Pran (2008) This short film created by the *New York Times* on the occasion of journalist Dith Pran's death in 2008 includes interviews with Pran and fellow journalist Sydney Schanberg.

S21: The Khmer Rouge Death Machine (2003) This documentary film examines the Tuol Sleng genocide prison through interviews with victims and guards.

Index